Explaining long-term economic change

New Studies in Economic and Social History

Edited for the Economic History Society by
Michael Sanderson
University of East Anglia, Norwich

This series, specially commissioned by the Economic History Society, provides a guide to the current interpretations of the key themes of economic and social history in which advances have recently been made or in which there has been significant debate.

In recent times economic and social history has been one of the most flourishing areas of historical study. This has mirrored the increasing relevance of the economic and social sciences both in a student's choice of career and in forming a society at large more aware of the importance of these issues in their everyday lives. Moreover specialist interests in business, agricultural and welfare history, for example, have themselves burgeoned and there has been an increased interest in the economic development of the wider world. Stimulating as these scholarly developments have been for the specialist, the rapid advance of the subject and the quantity of new publications make it difficult for the reader to gain an overview of particular topics, let alone the whole field.

New Studies in Economic and Social History is intended for students and their teachers. It is designed to introduce them to fresh topics and to enable them to keep abreast of recent writing and debates. All the books in the series are written by a recognised authority in the subject, and the arguments and issues are set out in a critical but unpartisan fashion. The aim of the series is to survey the current state of scholarship, rather than to provide a set of prepackaged conclusions.

The series has been edited since its inception in 1968 by Professors M. W. Flinn, T. C. Smout and L. A. Clarkson, and is currently edited by Dr Michael Sanderson. From 1968 it was published by Macmillan as *Studies in Economic History*, and after 1974 as *Studies in Economic and Social History*. From 1995 *New Studies in Economic and Social History* is being published on behalf of the Economic History Society by Cambridge University Press. This new series includes some of the titles previously published by Macmillan as well as new titles, and reflects the ongoing development throughout the world of this rich seam of history.

For a full list of titles in print, please see the end of the book.

Explaining long-term economic change

Prepared for the Economic History Society by

J. L. Anderson
La Trobe University, Melbourne

CAMBRIDGE
UNIVERSITY PRESS

Published by the Press Syndicate of the University of Cambridge
The Pitt Building, Trumpington Street, Cambridge CB2 1RP
40 West 20th Street, New York, NY 10011-4211, USA
10 Stamford Road, Oakleigh, Melbourne 3166, Australia

© The Economic History Society 1991
Explaining Long-Term Economic Change first published by
The Macmillan Press Limited 1991
First Cambridge University Press edition 1995

Printed in Great Britain at the University Press, Cambridge

A catalogue record for this book is available from the British Library

Library of Congress cataloguing in publication data

Anderson, J. L.
   Explaining long-term economic change / prepared for the Economic
History Society by J. L. Anderson. – 1st Cambridge University Press ed.
       p.   cm. – (New studies in economic and social history)
   Originally published: Hampshire: Macmillan Education, 1991. (New
studies in economic and social history).
   Includes bibliographical references and index.
   ISBN 0 521 55269 9 (hardcover). – ISBN 0 521 55784 4 (pbk.)
   1. Economic history. 2. Economics – History. 3. Business cycles.
I. Economic History Society. II. Title. III. Series.
HC51.A718   1995
338.5′4–dc20   95–4754
                                                                  CIP

ISBN 0 521 55269 9 hardback
ISBN 0 521 55784 4 paperback

CE

Contents

Acknowledgements

I should like to thank F. Anderson and L. Chai for their patience and support, M. Haviden for helpful comments and E. L. Jones whose enthusiasm, erudition and advice were indispensable.

Note on references

References in the text within brackets relate to items listed alphabetically in the Bibliography. Other references relate to notes grouped at the end of the text.

Introduction

A purpose of economic and social history is to explain how the world pattern of production and consumption has changed over time: in short, to contribute to an explanation of why some countries are rich while others are not.

To pursue this goal it is necessary to analyse how and why economic change occurs, and why the rate of change has differed at different times and in different places. Some scholars contribute to this in the traditional manner of historical research, through detailed studies of place or process. More and more, in economic history and also in historical sociology (Mennell, 1989), attempts are nowadays being made to synthesize these micro-histories into explanations of long-term economic change in large systems. This book examines important examples of these syntheses.

The scale at which the grand summaries have to be constructed requires that information be classified and aggregated. The relationships between these aggregates must then be structured in the form of models. These simplify reality; otherwise the mass of historical detail cannot be comprehended, the patterns discerned or causes identified.

In the models, aggregates are related in ways specified by theory, usually economic theory. This may be specific to narrowly defined problems in production, distribution or exchange, or applied more widely as in the theory of choice. The applied logic component of theory is seldom contentious but differences often arise over assumptions, over which aspects of an economy or society are important in a causal sense. Describing processes is less difficult than explaining why a process began.

Until relatively recently, the models most commonly relied on to provide both explanation of long-term change and a framework for detailed research were those of Karl Marx and Max Weber. As an abundant literature of exegesis, criticism and elaboration is devoted to the works of those scholars, Marxist and Weberian interpretations of history will only be touched on in this book.

The series of explanations reviewed in the following chapters are each built around an important determinant of long-term economic and social change. The discussion of each approach reviews its strengths and weaknesses, although the coverage is of course not exhaustive. Further, the models are not given equal space. Those in which economic analysis is most prominent are discussed more fully because of both their importance to the explanation of economic change and the need to provide adequate detail on their theoretical elements.

To meet the requirement of brevity, many major works are outlined here in a few sentences. Some lengthy debates are summarized in a few phrases. The process of condensation and abridgement has eliminated all of the caveats, qualifications and nuances that appear in the works selected for study and in the detailed commentaries published on them. For the guidance of those who wish to acquire a deeper understanding of the models, a readily accessible work of interpretation has sometimes been cited together with that of the seminal work. Bibliographies in these interpretations in turn provide an *entrée* into the literature surrounding the particular model, explanation or problem.

It is not possible in a work of distillation to cite the sources of every item of information, idea or interpretation without risking the citations exceeding the length of the text. Many of the points raised have passed into the common knowledge of economists, historians, and scholars in cognate disciplines. This makes attribution honorific rather than functional. The origins of ideas mentioned in the text will become readily apparent to the student reading more deeply on any of the topics. Some citations have been used as signposts for further reading and thus it would not be helpful to specify page numbers.

Social scientists typically aggregate their data to analyse change in large systems. By contrast, historians generally base their explanations on a detailed assessment of primary sources, which necessarily restricts the scope of the inquiry in time and place.

Accordingly, historians often look askance at theories of history, or even at explanations of long-term change. However, these explanations are really to be thought of as aggregations of the available micro-histories and, since these generalized explanations of the past affect people's understanding of the modern world, they are the most widely influential aspects of the discipline. They are not in principle at odds with works of deep scholarship; rather they aim to put them together to provide a context in which their significance can be understood.

People will in any case continue to construct and be influenced by a 'world view' that is partly based on their perception of the pattern of the past over wide areas and long periods. It is preferable that their view be informed by knowledge and tempered by caution concerning the problems of understanding long-term change. This book provides an introduction to a variety of models, theories or explanations dealing with long-term change, of varying degrees of plausibility, robustness and value. A proper acquaintance with these should reduce the chance that we will form our opinions on world history casually – as the unwitting prisoners of some unknown theoretician or philosopher.

1
Models, theories and history

History on a simple view is the story of past events. More usefully defined, history is an inquiry, involving both evidence and explanation, or in the terminology of the sciences, data and theory. Without explanation, the other two elements of a historical presentation have little value; narration becomes chronicle and description antiquarianism.

Inquiries at different levels of detail require different methods. The conventional approach to explanation in what might be termed micro-history is to examine, assess and evaluate all the documents or other primary sources bearing on a problem, and from that evidence to construct a story of conditions, processes and causes. This method serves well for investigations of problems narrowly bounded in time and in space; but in order to explain change in the very long term and in large social units, a different approach is required. In studies of societies rather than individuals and of change extending over centuries rather than years or decades, reliance has necessarily to be placed on secondary sources; while to comprehend the wealth of information available and to provide plausible explanations for the changes observed, recourse must be had to the techniques offered by the social sciences, particularly the use of explicit theory and the construction of models.

The logical status of 'models' needs to be grasped. Within a model, the complexity of social experience is reduced to manageable proportions for analytical and explanatory purposes (McClelland, 1975). Models in the social sciences are intellectual constructs in which reality is simplified without significant distortion. This is achieved by categorizing data on the basis of some common property and then relating the categories by causal hypotheses. As the structure is based on the statistical regularities observed in the aggregate behaviour of large numbers of units, conclusions drawn from a model can be expressed only in terms of probabilistic tendency, not of certainty. This technique of selection, abstraction and aggregation permits the isolation of key variables and the analysis of causation. As such, it is appropriate to the study of economic change in large systems.

All models can be assessed in two ways: by asking whether their construction is logical and by testing their assumptions and conclusions against the reality which they purport to represent. However, scholars in their pursuit of realism can and do differ in their choices of initial conditions and in their assessments of what constitute valid and useful behavioural assumptions. At one extreme of opinion about behaviour, formalists assume that economic laws apply universally with respect to time and place, while at the other extreme, substantivists argue that each society must be studied wholly within the terms of its own structure and functioning. The appropriateness of either of these perspectives may be judged by reference to the nature of and constraints upon economic activity. These constraints depend in large part on the length of time encompassed by the study: the longer the period, the greater the probability that social restrictions will be modified or loosened to give wider scope for the so-called economic motives, particularly income or wealth maximization.

In conventional historical writing, models are seldom specified or even made explicit. Yet the necessary abstraction, the process of selection of items of evidence that is required by historical scholarship, presupposes the existence of at least some framework of inquiry, a world-view or paradigm – an 'implicit body of intertwined theoretical and methodological belief that permits selection, evaluation, and criticism' (Kuhn, 1970: *17*). 'Facts' become historical facts only when invested with significance by some preconceived if highly generalized structure of explanation or philosophy of history (Carr, 1964). While accepting the need for accuracy and comprehensiveness, few historians would nowadays go on to accept the position of the nineteenth-century German scholar Ranke that 'what actually happened' can be independently established, with the interpretation of those happenings then becoming self-evident and unique. The arrangement of the data into a coherent, consistent explanation in other than a *post hoc ergo propter hoc* way requires behavioural assumptions derived from some theory of human conduct, however covert. These assumptions are often based on perceptions of 'common sense', and concealed in simple assertions of cause and effect.

In the analysis of long-term change in large systems, models structured on economic history have been found to be of singular relevance. Economic forces can in time act to overcome various social and political constraints. Further, as economics is characteristically concerned with the aggregate effect of individuals' actions, rather than with the actions of an individual, it lends itself to the analysis of the operation of large systems. Moreover, in a study of long-term change, we need to look at changes in activities such as procreation, production, distribution and consumption – aspects of life that have been of overwhelming importance to most people throughout time. Economic theory in its assumptions, method and content has been developed precisely to analyse these activities.

Neoclassical economics, which is broadly consonant with microeconomics, offers a useful and generalizable theory of choice and allocation. This body of theory rests on two assumptions. The first is of rationality, that individuals can order preferences and will endeavour to act in their self-interest to choose more rather than less of a desirable commodity or service. This analysis of choice and allocation based on the assumption of rationality is *not* confined to market situations or market-dominated societies. A problem in military tactics or strategy for example, being one of choice and resource allocation, is also amenable to the analysis.

The assumption of rationality does not require that all members of a population at all times singlemindedly endeavour to maximize material gain. In dealing with problems at the scale of long-term change in large systems, economic theory can generally offer only first approximations, explanations of trend. Even a formal economic model contains an error term that allows for unspecified factors such as changing social and political constraints on choice, or socially determined objectives not associated with income maximization. The Hindu caste system is an extreme case of social and economic constraint, but even that is malleable, given time. More generally, over the long term and with large numbers, the aggregate outcome of individuals' actions will tend to be *as if* wealth maximization had been the goal, although social and political structures not leading directly to this may nevertheless persist for long periods (Basu *et al.*, 1987; Olson, 1982). The second basic assumption of economic theory is that group behaviour has a central tendency: although individuals differ, their actions in aggregate can be conceived of as being normally distributed around a mean or average. Changes over time can be described and analysed in terms of the average, however much the actions of any single individual may differ from that norm. This assumption of the central tendency of large numbers does not deny that the behaviour of some individuals has been uniquely important in its apparent effect on the course of history. No theory can account for a Genghis Khan, a Peter the Great, or, as is usually mentioned in this context, the effect on Roman history of the shape of Cleopatra's nose! Chance in history must be recognized and the estimation of its importance must remain as a matter of judgement.

Even when non-economic forces are decisive, economic analysis can still contribute to historical understanding. It can isolate areas of a problem that call for analysis using techniques other than those of economic theory. With initial conditions specified, an economic model can indicate the expected outcome of change in given variables; and with the hypothetical outcome as a reference-point, deviations from it in the historical record can be identified and their explanations sought. Economic theory predicts, for example, that labour scarcity will lead to a rise in price of that factor of production and a shift in income distribution toward labour. This happened in Western Europe after the Black Death. However, when the outcome of labour scarcity was *not* gain to the peasants but the burdens of serfdom, as in the tenth century and in the sixteenth century in Eastern Europe, a different explanation must be sought. The analysis must be extended. The lords' effective monopoly of force out-weighed the importance conferred on the peasants by their scarcity in these particular cases (Brenner, 1985).

Nevertheless, while neoclassical economic theory is useful in explaining the allocation of goods, factors of production and services, and how change in one variable may affect others, it cannot explain the origin of change. Accordingly, economic models that are presented as explaining long-term or secular change have characteristically been based on changes in other factors – in resources, population, ideology or technology.

Technical change is fundamental to the most widely known explanation of historical change, that offered by Karl Marx. The Marxist formulation is less an example of the use of theory *in* history than an example of a theory *of* history, with consequent claims of comprehensiveness and inevitability. Baldly summarized, the model is that the historically continuous process of improvement in technology leads to tension between classes which are defined by their members' degree of control over the means of production. The development of new techniques means that the political and social 'superstructure' is no longer appropriate to the way goods and services can be produced. This tension is resolved by a revolution which establishes a new power structure in society appropriate to the new ways of production. Thus with the growth of trade and industry the feudal lords were obliged to give way to the capitalists (bourgeoisie). They in their turn are to be overthrown by the workers (proletariat), a propertyless class created by the activities of the capitalists themselves. The accumulation of capital in Marx's model impoverishes all but a few, while the proletariat is drilled and disciplined as a revolutionary army by the repetitious work and regimented regime in the capitalists' factories.

The Marxist model can be rejected for many reasons: theoretical, historical (Conway, 1987) and political. The nature and inevitability of the historical process and its outcome in the Marxist schema are unacceptable to the historians who emphasize both the contingent in history and the problems of defining operationally a number of concepts central to the model, such as 'class'. It is argued that stages of 'feudalism' and 'capitalism' can be found universally only by the most strained interpretations of the historical record. Moreover, the Marxist theory is perceived as having failed to predict the direction of historical development, let alone its timing. Politically, many see the culmination of Marxist dialectic not in universal freedom and prosperity with a withering away of the coercive state as predicted by Marx, but in an oppressive and grossly inefficient state capitalism and stagnation in industrial societies, and in a grinding and persisting poverty in areas of the less developed world.

Accordingly, many scholars have turned their minds away from the insights offered in Marx's method and writings, to concentrate in the more conventional way on historical problems specific to place and time. Unfortunately, in so doing they ignore the great issue in historical studies: how to put the pieces together, the necessary prelude to explaining why the world is as it is. However, a few have offered alternative theories of history. Rostow's formulation is one of these, explicitly 'a non-communist manifesto' (Rostow, 1960).

Rostow's theory of history is one of successive stages of development, identified largely but not entirely by economic criteria, the decisive stage being that in which there is a relatively rapid 'take-off' into self-sustained economic growth. This stages theory enjoyed considerable popularity amongst economists and others impressed with its apparent rigour, even though its conceptual and empirical foundations were the subjects of immediate and sustained critical controversy (Rostow, 1964). The central concept of the 'take-off' was, however, less misleading in analysis than in its rhetorically implicit promise to poor countries of a brief and imminent twenty-year take-off period.

A close analysis of Rostow's model offers little cause for euphoria. If the three stages between the 'traditional society' and the 'age of high mass consumption' are considered – preconditions, take-off and drive to maturity – about a century would pass before a poor society could expect to enjoy the fruits of development. Further, this assumes contrary to fact that undeveloped countries in the modern world are at the institutional and material level that characterized Britain in the eighteenth century, the place and time of the first 'take-off'. While in the 1960s a conscious conflation of conditions in pre-industrial Britain and third world countries may have seemed to make Industrial Revolution studies more relevant to the problems of development (Deane, 1965), it was already being urged that nations in Europe had developed and logically must have developed in different ways at different times. The reason for the different patterns of development was the differing degrees of economic backwardness in some states relative to those that had already industrialized (Gerschenkron, 1962).

These formulations and the models discussed in the following chapters are based on the belief that the events of history can be seen as patterns which may be analysed partly or largely in terms of the behaviour of human groups engaged in the processes of production, distribution and consumption. On this foundation, the models offer explanations of how things came to be as they are. They provide insights that can in turn provide a better understanding of conditions in the present. From that understanding purposeful policies may be developed.

Insights into the process of change in the past can also inform judgements about the likely course of events in the future. Of course prediction, in the sense of precise description of future events, is not possible. However, forecasting is. As part of daily life, every individual is constantly engaged in forecasting, that is to say, in making probabilistic guesses about some aspect of future events. The more the guesses are informed by a knowledge of why things are as they are and what forces tend to bring about changes, the more accurate are the guesses likely to be. A necessary element of that knowledge is an understanding of how and why events occurred in the past.

Just as an individual relies largely on memory for purposive action, so a society must rely on history, its collective memory. This is well understood by totalitarian regimes. Application of the maxim, 'who controls the past controls the future: who controls the present controls the past' (Orwell, 1954: *31*) has unfortunately not been confined to fiction. Szporluk (1986) writes of official control of history in the USSR in this century. In China, two thousand years ago, among the steps taken by the first emperor to unify the states he had conquered was the destruction of their written histories, the written memory of their separate identities.

What follows, then, is a review of a number of models that have been offered to answer the question of compelling importance in the study of both history and economics: why some societies increased their material welfare over time, while others did not.

2
Market explanations of economic change

Adam Smith in *The Wealth of Nations* (1776) provided a singularly durable model of economic growth based on analysis of production and market exchange. Markets are networks of buyers and sellers who negotiate the exchange of commodities, the prices determined between buyers and sellers determining the nature and quantities of goods and services offered and sought. A market need not be confined to a particular place, but may be the expression of communication between scattered buyers and sellers. A market system may be taken to exist when a substantial proportion of commodities consumed in a society are acquired by sale and purchase rather than produced and consumed within a household.

Smith's model is based on an assumption of the primacy of self-interest as a force motivating individuals, a by-product being a universal propensity to 'truck, barter, and exchange' (Smith, 1776: *17*). The process of exchange makes possible a division of labour that in turn raises productivity. Division of labour, or in more general terms, specialization in the process of production, allows producers to concentrate on tasks for which they have a natural aptitude, saves time and capital, and over time facilitates the acquisition of skills and fosters inventiveness. Accordingly, although each individual may be seeking only his or her advantage, by competing in a free market each will be led, 'as if by an invisible hand', to benefit society at large (Smith, 1776: *477*). Individuals in pursuing their own interests also make provision for future increases in production by saving. This saving, or abstinence from consumption, makes possible the accumulation of capital goods – defined as the produced means of production – and so provides for an increase in output over time. In this way, through the self-regulating mechanism of a free market, a nation's wealth can be secured and expanded.

In Smith's perception, government intervention in the market process is largely counter-productive. It distorts the pattern of production otherwise dictated by the preferences of producers and consumers freely expressed in the market. The role he allows to government is to provide defence, law and order, and some vaguely specified public instruction. The tacit and explicit mutual support that grew up between merchants and the state in early modern Europe, a relationship later called mercantilism, was anathema to Smith.

Smith's analysis was concerned with change over time, whereas much of modern theory dealing with the market is static, concerned primarily with the efficient allocation of resources and commodities at any one time. Modern models of growth developed within this framework are variations on the theme of the relationship between saving, investment and output over time under restrictive assumptions (*vide* Hahn and Matthews, 1964). They do not incorporate the structural change – organizational and institutional – which characterizes sustained growth in the long term. Smith's purpose was to analyse and explain this form of economic growth or, more generally, development.

Economic development is based on three conditions: the provision of incentives for individuals to engage in productive activity, a responsive system of supply of goods and services, and a concentration of demand. Smith argues that the market fulfils all three requirements.

The market offers ready opportunity and powerful inducement to an individual to increase his or her productivity. The hope of gain and fear of loss that are associated with market activity provide constant incentive for economic units to produce, to use resources efficiently, to innovate, to save and to invest. The incentives spring from the impersonal reward system: gain or loss are linked to the extent to which a producer can satisfy demand expressed in the market, through the skill, imagination, energy and resources embodied in the goods or services that he or she supplies. As well as fostering productive activity, the market can also effect more conservation than many of its critics admit, provided that property rights are clearly specified and enforced. The excesses of resource exploitation or creation of nuisance often attributed to the operation of the market can more properly be ascribed to a failure of legislators to establish the legal conditions necessary to bring the cost to individuals of their actions closer to the cost to society, or to reduce open access resources to specified ownership or control.

The market is a disaggregated system of economic control and co-ordination which permits rapid adjustment of production patterns to incorporate new techniques or to meet new demands. These changes are necessarily, indeed definitionally, part of the process of economic development: growth in output cannot be sustained in the long term without changes in the structure of the economy. In a market system, decision-making is not the province of some central authority, but is vested in individuals, firms and households. This is, in aggregate, a form of insurance against the consequences of economic error and a means by which best practice techniques can be disseminated. An efficient decision will be copied by other economic units; an inefficient decision will inflict loss on the unit involved but will generally have little effect on the wider economy. This contrasts with the operation of command structures, wherein an error at the centre of control necessarily affects the whole system. Again in contrast to a command system, the market does not require arduous co-ordination of production with its associated costs and inefficiencies. Market prices provide an effective feedback of information, by means of which consumers and producers can adjust their behaviour.

By concentrating demand and providing the opportunity for exchange, a market permits an individual, firm or region to increase productivity by specialization. The division of labour emphasized by Smith is one aspect of this. Concentration upon an activity in which even an inefficient unit has a *comparative* advantage over other units brings improved productivity through, for example, technical development and the cost-reducing benefits of economies of scale. Accordingly, increasing wealth through specialization and trade definitely need not rest upon the exploitation of one participant by another. In addition to increasing production, trade can allow the diversification of consumption: consumers can be presented with a wider choice of commodities and services, allowing their wants to be more fully satisfied. The process of exchange is demonstrably *not* a zero-sum activity.

Given the importance of trade and markets in increasing output, it is not surprising that historical accounts of economic change in the long term often have a Smithian underpinning, with economic development accompanying a widening of the market (Holton, 1985: *32*). The story of European progress is an example. The relative autarky of the feudal manor gave way in the eleventh century to buying and selling at fairs. When the quantities of goods demanded and supplied permitted regular and settled trading, fairs were superseded by towns as centres of commerce. The trickle of goods flowing between towns developed into networks of local, regional and long-distance trade, the last of these often controlled by great chartered or joint-stock companies.

The market model of progress based on competing units is a powerful explanatory device; indeed, it is sufficiently powerful to carry a weight of historical explanation by analogy. For instance, the functioning of the European states-system can be analysed as if the states were firms operating in a competitive market (Jones, 1981). Both firms and states, whatever their resources and forms of management or government, compete with others of their kind. Those that are inefficient, or possibly unlucky, disappear from the system, their assets not lost but taken over by other units. This effects a system-wide improvement in efficiency, provided that no firm or state gains a monopoly position.

However useful, the model in itself cannot explain development. The existence of markets, or even of a market system, affords no guarantee of continued economic expansion. Smith was well aware of this and offered China and Bengal as examples of stagnation and decline respectively (Smith, 1776: *80*, *82*). A developed market system certainly need not lead to industrialization, as is demonstrated on the grandest scale by the failure in China to build on the proto-industrial revolution of the Song dynasty of the tenth to thirteenth centuries (Elvin, 1973; Jones, 1988).

Among those directly in the Smithian tradition, Sir John Hicks, Nobel Laureate in economics, is the most prominent. His model is the most useful illustration of the nature, strengths and weaknesses of explanations of historical change based on the theory of the market (Hicks, 1969). Hicks analyses economic implications of the rise, development and spread of markets for commodities and factors. The presentation is positive, that is, classificatory and explanatory, but it also has a normative purpose: he bases policy prescriptions on his reading of history.

Hicks necessarily directs his analysis of history to 'the group, not the individual', and tries to explain 'the average, or norm, of the group' (*p. 3*). This, as he correctly says, 'is what we do, almost all the time, in economics'. He tests explanations in the model by relatively casual reference to the historical record, 'so as to see that we do not put our logical processes into a form which clashes with the largest and most obvious facts' (*p. 8*). This way of proceeding has attracted strong scholarly criticism: there is no specification of which facts would verify the hypothesis, which are irrelevant exceptions, and which would refute it (Bauer, 1971). Further, quite important categories are stretched to cover a wide variety of social entities often dissimilar in form and function – Hicks's assumptions of an essential uniformity among city-states and among colonies are examples. These criticisms do not, however, vitiate the model. As it operates at an extremely high degree of abstraction, its persuasiveness or otherwise must be largely intuitive. In economics, propositions may depend for their acceptance less on rigorous scientific 'proofs' than on the quality of the 'rhetoric' in which they are presented (McCloskey, 1985).

Although Hicks speaks of 'statistical uniformity', his model is not based on inductive reasoning: indeed, given its temporal and geographical scope it could not be. Instead, he proceeds deductively by specifying initial conditions, historical phenomena, and then uses economic theory to deduce their implications. He begins with the 'rise of the market, the rise of the exchange economy' and then sees 'what logically follows from it' (*p. 7*). The chief weakness in this approach is that given the level of generality at which the initial conditions must be specified, and the range of exogenous forces affecting the process, various effects might be the logical result of any given cause. Merchants faced with falling profits, for example, may engage in armed conflict, in collusion and market sharing, or in market expansion and product innovation. Each of these three options has different consequences for the history of economic progress. This uncertainty is acceptable only if, as in this case, the aim of the model is to explain rather than predict.

Explanations of this kind remain useful and testable against the evidence. The value of 'explanatory' models lies in their ability to indicate why one economic event should have been followed by another. Indeed, economic theory is designed to specify causal relationships between sequential events.

The core of Hicks's model is the rise of the market, the development of the mercantile or commercial economy, which he perceives as having been expressed historically in three stages or 'phases'. These phases are essentially analytical categories, applied at any appropriate point with scant regard for chronology.

The first phase is the emergence of commercial exchange, and the development of that process within the city-state. The trade and specialist traders that are central to the model have their origins in the non-market 'revenue economy' structured on principles of custom or command. Trade grows and specialized traders emerge. The development of this specialization of function is seen as the consequence of peasants disposing of output which is surplus to their needs, the surreptitious trade of state officials, and the legitimate activities of those primarily engaged in brigandage and piracy. In this process, the city-state, defined as a creature of trade and traders, is of central importance (*p. 41*). Economic historians have long ascribed the same origin and function to European towns. In a relatively small society to some extent dependent on foreign trade, merchants could achieve a status denied to them in large, pre-industrial agrarian systems. Accordingly, the town or city-state became a mercantile enclave as the merchant-citizens fashioned its institutions of government to their purposes. The conditions necessary for the functioning of a market system were established: protection of property and enforcement of contract.

Hicks's second or middle phase is characterized by the survival of trading centres within a quasi-mercantile imperial state, which is itself further commercialized by its ingestion of the city-states. In this context commercial law is codified and increasingly accepted, forms of private and public finance are developed, and land and labour become marketable commodities. The Industrial Revolution in turn can be viewed as 'a continuation of the process of mercantile development' (*p. 143*).

Despite the indifference to chronology and emphasis on process in the specification of the first and second phases, the third phase – the modern phase – is comprehensively defined by a temporal criterion: 'the state the world is in at the present day' (*p. 160*). The sequential processes of relevance have presumably been completed; the spread of modern, high-productivity technique is to be studied as a lateral process.

The answer to the question of why the poor of the underdeveloped world cannot be readily absorbed into the industrial sector, as some were in the past, is found by Hicks to lie in an 'administrative revolution' within government that occurred early in the present century. This permitted the partial reinstatement of the 'revenue economy': the state regulation, domination or control of the economic system. The state, it is argued, once again can and does frustrate the potential for growth inherent in the free market. Policy prescription follows from the model: trade should be freed, the state presumably should retire to its limited, Smithian place. The prescription is simple, but to the point of being simplistic. Conclusions drawn from the analysis are not modified to allow for the contextual contrasts between the twentieth century and the preceding millennia, nor is the state allowed a positive role in the process of economic development.

Focusing on the virtues of the market, Hicks is dismissive of the activities of early modern states. He mentions the attempts by governments in the seventeenth and eighteenth centuries to promote economic growth in the national interest, and asserts but does not demonstrate that 'this first mercantilism was a failure' (*p. 162*). However, while the policies and practices of those states were often inept, their purpose was generally sound. The broad objectives of mercantilist policy were profit and power, which together represent a fairly crude but functional definition of economic development at a time of incessant struggle between those early nations for markets and resources. The more soundly based mercantilist policies went toward creating, expanding and protecting areas in which the fragile market could operate and develop (Wilson, 1965:269; Rostow, 1975).

Mercantilism was an expression of the mutually beneficial or symbiotic relationship that existed between rulers and the commercial sector in European nation states. It contrasts strikingly with the parasitic relationship characteristic of despotic oriental empires, the contrast going far to account for the differential performance of the two types of systems (Jones, 1981). The economic backwardness of nations early in their development appeared to call for a greater role for the state in the promotion of trade and industry than is suggested by presentations based on *laissez faire* theory and on the post-mercantilist experience of Britain, the first industrial nation (Gerschenkron, 1962).

Among the many valuable insights offered by Hicks's model, two stand out: the importance of the development of factor markets and the pressure on traders to innovate. Adam Smith adequately described the importance of commodity markets, but the further, crucial step toward development lay in bringing into the market the factors of production, notably land and labour. Resistance to their commercialization turned upon their importance within non-market structures of social custom or political power, but, until they could be traded freely, entrepreneurs were restricted in the extent to which they could acquire and combine them in new and more productive ways.

With such new combinations of factors, the market further expanded and gave entrepreneurs the opportunity to innovate, while imposing penalties upon them if they did not do so. The opportunities of an expanding market were obvious; the penalties imposed were perhaps less so, but none the less effective. As the volume of trade in a commodity or a given market increased or, as new entrants were attracted, costs would tend to rise and prices fall, reducing profit margins. As the merchants' essential function is earning profits and reinvesting them, response to a fall in profit is likely to be trade in a new commodity or in a new area. These innovations will increase the scale and scope of the market and raise productivity. In Hicks's view they can also lead to the development of industry (*p. 144*).

However, as noted earlier, merchants when faced with damaging competition may not respond in a way beneficial to the economy. They have often chosen instead to engage in warfare or, more commonly in recent times, in some form of collusive market-sharing arrangement. Warfare would be likely on aggregate to result in net economic loss. Market sharing, by eliminating competition, eliminates much of the dynamic of the market system. Adam Smith remarked on merchants' taste for avoiding competition in the market: 'people of the same trade seldom meet together, even for merriment and diversion, but the conversation ends in a conspiracy against the public, or in some contrivance to raise prices' (Smith I: *144*).

Market models can elucidate important historical processes but cannot represent comprehensive theories of history. In Hicks's model, for example, non-economic factors are not incorporated even when their economic importance is accepted. Political and military events shape the nature and timing of the phases, but are themselves unexplained. Again, religion, considered by Weber (1904; Collins, 1986) and Tawney (1938) among others to have been of crucial significance, is mentioned (*p. 167*) but is treated as if it were dependent on economic forces. What is more, although explaining an absence of development in areas beyond Europe is a chief purpose of Hicks's model, the histories of those areas receive scant attention in it. More generally, geographic factors, upon which, for example, the analysis of city-states turns at one remove (*p. 38*) are inadequately incorporated. It is to a consideration of models which deal explicitly with elements of geography as it affects economic development that we now turn.

3
The environment

Analysis of economic change cannot exclude consideration of the natural environment within which decisions are made. Geography, in the words of Braudel, 'helps us to rediscover the slow unfolding of structural realities, to see things in the perspective of the very long term' (Braudel, 1975: *23*). Even Hicks's 'market' model is based ultimately upon geographic factors, but the introduction of these elements into his analysis is *ad hoc*: they are treated as incidental to his main theme, the development of the market. However, other historical accounts embrace aspects of geography more systematically, placing them at the heart of explanation.

The physical and biological environment is often treated as a constant that helps to account for the failure of certain regions to progress economically. The patterns of life in the hot and cold deserts of the world and on their margins are examples of environmental influence, even control. In the tropical world, the infertility of the soil and endemic diseases are constraints which have tended to limit the production of a surplus that could be used for investment and so for development. However, in order to account for change, either the environment itself must change, as climate has done, or some new technique or social activity must change the set of opportunities and constraints. The latter is the implicit basis of Wittfogel's model (1957). In this, dependence upon irrigation explains the origin and stability of certain oriental systems – the so called 'hydraulic civilizations'.

To Wittfogel, the foundation of 'oriental despotism' is an environment that obliges a society to depend on a base of irrigation agriculture. The need for co-ordination of the public works necessary for large-scale irrigation and the allocation of water rights in such a system requires strong centralized direction. In order to receive this the peasants had necessarily to surrender their freedoms to a central authority. This has some relevance to Mesopotamia and Egypt, but considerably less to China, where the form of despotic rule was observable but did not have this function. China was ruled by bureaucratic inertia; in reality the initiatives for irrigation development and co-ordination of rights and activities were largely at the local level (Stover and Stover, 1976). Moreover, China was not the static, changeless economy that the hydraulic theory would require. Spectacular technical and economic development was achieved under the Song dynasty (McNeill, 1982). The model is still less relevant to India, much of which is reliant on the monsoon for agricultural production rather than on extensive and elaborate hydraulic works.

However, most grand models do capture some aspect of reality and there is a kernel of truth in Wittfogel's formulation. The great river valleys are regions in which a physiographic and cultural unity made political unification and domination by a warlord relatively easy. Further, the high agricultural productivity of the extensive, well-watered alluvial soils provided taxes to support civilizations and their systems of administration – and repression. This contrasts with Europe, where areas of good agricultural land that yielded large tax revenues were not contiguous. This pattern influenced the formation of separate political entities in Europe, the nation-states (Pounds and Ball, 1964). The diversified and dispersed resources of Europe were also an encouragement to specialization and trade. This is a further contrast with the great river valleys of Asia, where more uniform production meant that distance trade tended to be restricted to luxuries. There, trade and traders were relatively easily controlled by political authorities.

Site and location are obvious facts of geography affecting the development of a system. History has many examples of economies that have flourished because they lay on trade routes, or commanded some important resource. Yet, trade patterns and the value of a 'resource' are themselves determined by the nature of technology and the level of development as it affects carriers and traded commodities. Indeed, resources are defined by the technology which enables them to be used. For example, flint was a resource of singular importance only to the stone-age hunters of the palaeolithic era, while mineral oil became a valuable resource only with the refining of kerosene for lamps and the development of the internal combustion engine. Further, neither favourable location for trade nor abundant natural resources is a necessary condition for economic development, as the history of Japan strikingly demonstrates.

The benefits of a location favourable in military terms have been important to the development of some states, and even to their survival. The Dutch Republic and Constantinople (Istanbul), as instances, benefited from being at nodal points on trade routes and in defensible locations. The success of the Dutch in their eighty-year struggle against the military might of Spain in the sixteenth and seventeenth centuries owed much to the profitability of their seaborne commerce and to the defensive barriers formed by the waterways of their land. Constantinople was well sited tactically on the Golden Horn and strategically on the Bosphorus. If blockaded by sea its citizens could draw resources from the Balkans or Anatolia, while if the city were attacked by land they could receive supplies by ship from the Black Sea or Mediterranean. On a larger scale, the off-shore locations of both Britain and Japan enabled them to draw technical and cultural inspiration from their powerful continental neighbours without being overwhelmed by them.

The environment has one seductive quality as an element in an explanatory scheme: even if the magnitude of the effect is seldom measurable, the direction of causation is usually clear. Of all the elements of the environment, climate is that in which the direction of causation is (historically) unambiguous. In addition, climate has demonstrably changed in historical times. This has led some to find in climatic change a decisive (though not necessarily deter-mining) element of economic change and a powerful influence on history itself.

The climatic model has generally been presented as one in which long-term climatic amelioration or deterioration slackens or tightens the environmental constraints upon agrarian productivity, and in this way affects the economy, society, and the course of historical change (e.g. Lamb, 1982; Bryson and Murray, 1977). The logic of the model is that just as the weather has a powerful influence on any given harvest, so it may be assumed that climatic change will produce long-term trends in output. However, although the sensitivity of plant growth to meteorological conditions means that climatic change must have had some agronomic and hence economic effects, the effects on the historical pattern are difficult to isolate (de Vries, 1981).

The relationship between incremental changes in climate and long-term trends in economic indicators cannot be deductively specified, as there is no historically unique effect of any given change over time in climatic parameters. That is to say, an amelioration of the climate is permissive only: nothing need result from it. A deterioration certainly restricts production, but the response is not predictable. Members of an affected society may adjust by altering their farming practices, may simply become poorer, or perhaps through discoveries made in meeting the challenge they may move to a higher level of productivity. This indeterminance is the fundamental weakness of Toynbee's 'challenge and response' model of historical change (Toynbee, 1934). There is indeed no way to specify in advance the kind of response, if any, that will be made to a particular 'challenge'. All the alternative ways of adjusting to climatic deterioration involve higher costs but there is generally no way of separating the adjustments from those caused by changes in other forces.

Climatic interpretations based on the inductive method have been no more satisfactory, although in attempts to draw conclusions from a mass of data some correlations between indices of climatic changes and social changes have been observed (Galloway, 1986). Thus climatic amelioration early in the current millennium coincided with the medieval expansion of population, towns and trade. The warming reached a maximum about 1200 AD. A period of colder winters and less reliable rainfall followed. This culminated in the 'Little Ice Age' that ran from about the mid sixteenth to the mid eighteenth century, with its most intense phase in the seventeenth century. The cooling, caused by changed wind circulation patterns, coincided with population decline until the seventeenth century famines, epidemics, wars and economic depressions supposedly produced a 'General Crisis' in Europe. At the other end of the Eurasian landmass, China was experiencing the convulsions associated with the fall of the Ming dynasty and the Manchu invasion.

The broad contemporaneity of these physical and historical

events, within and beyond Europe, has lent support to a model in which climate is the chief determinant of the economic and historical trends. That model is based on a 'supply-side' interpretation of economic events, in which changes stem from variations in production. It neglects the fluctuations in demand brought about by demographic movements, themselves broadly explicable in terms of population growth, with disease as a major influence.

Changes in demand associated with population change offer more convincing explanations for trends in agricultural output in Europe than does climatic change. The agricultural crisis of the late fourteenth and fifteenth centuries – falling grain prices and land abandonment – has been ascribed to the increasing cold and wetness of the climate in that period (Steensberg, 1951: *672*). Yet the *fall* in agricultural prices indicates that over the period the supply of food exceeded the demand of a population diminished by plague, whereas a worsening climate would have caused prices to rise. The contraction of the area farmed was the result of this fall in demand for food, not the result of climatic deterioration shifting the physical margin of cultivation. Again, when climate was deteriorating in the sixteenth century, grain yields in Europe were increasing through the improvement in farming induced by the pressure of a growing population and rising prices (Slicher van Bath, 1977: *82*). Examples can be multiplied (Anderson, 1981).

An overarching climatic model of historical change remains at the level of intriguing hypothesis. Certainly, marginal agricultural areas may be affected, but peoples at the margins of cultivation are generally themselves marginal to historical trends. The Viking irruption was a significant movement, but the reasons for that probably have more to do with the development of ironworking and shipbuilding and the attractions of rich and poorly defended shores and river valleys. The Mongols were certainly significant in the histories of almost all of the agricultural societies on the periphery of the central Asian steppe lands, perhaps decisively so in terms of political and economic developments following their conquests (Jones, 1988). However, climatic trends in inner Asia remain too obscure to explain the cycles of nomad aggression.

An alternative approach to assessing the effect of the historical importance of climate, or of the environment generally, is to consider the nature and degree of risk to which a society is exposed. The impact of natural and social disasters appears to have been lighter in European than in Asian societies, and within Europe seems to have fallen disproportionately upon people rather than on capital works and equipment. This bias in the nature of shocks suffered by Europeans – a sort of 'neutron bomb' effect – may have offered a small but cumulative advantage to Europeans in terms of capital accumulation and hence in productivity. At the same time, the 'insurance' function of large families in the relatively risky Asian environments would have tended to foster more rapid population growth, thus further adversely affecting the ratio of labour to capital (Jones, 1981; Anderson and Jones, 1988). In addition, because the incidence of natural disasters falls disproportionately upon the poor, who can least afford risk-management strategies, a high risk environment will tend to increase inequalities of income distribution. Those with the greatest command over resources are most likely to survive disasters and to profit from them as well. More generally, part of the divergence in the characteristics and performances of the economies of Russia and the United States of America can be accounted for by the differing risks, both natural and political, to which each society was exposed (White, 1987).

Research on the nature and intensity of environmental shocks as a cause of change is relatively recent. The link between climatic and historical change has conventionally been sought in a sequence where climate affects harvests, these affect the economy, and this in turn affects social actions. This approach has produced no persuasive result, largely because of independent or unpredictable changes in the variables intervening between climatic and social change. Chief among these is population. While the environment may impose fixed or variable constraints on population numbers at a particular time, disease has been a major determinant of population size within the limits set by the environment. To demonstrate a causal relationship between climatic and demographic trends, it would seem that it is necessary to establish a relationship between the effects of climatic change and mortality caused by disease.

Disease organisms and their vectors require specific ranges of temperature and humidity to function. Studies have shown that disease mortality can be closely correlated with seasonal conditions – notably summer drought and winter cold. But the results cannot at this stage be confidently extrapolated to yield conclusions for the long term (Lee, 1981: *396*). The virulence of diseases of major demographic significance – plague and smallpox – has not been shown to be influenced by secular climatic change (Appleby, 1981).

The environment, whether static or changing, does not determine change, but rather provides a society with sets of opportunities and constraints. These are not immutable. They are perhaps best thought of as having an effect on a society's cost structure and through that on levels of consumption and investment. These effects are partly dependent upon the society's social, economic and technical development; and on the extent to which the ratio of population to resources has rendered the economy vulnerable to environmental change. Population dynamics and technical levels are themselves the foundations of other models of long-term economic change.

4

Population: the importance of people

Few models of long-term change do not at least implicitly incorp-orate some reference to demographic factors. This reflects the importance of people: production depends on people, the purpose of economic activity is consumption by people, and change in the number of people influences economic and social change. Unfor-tunately, the relationship between population change and other changes is seldom simple; models that incorporate population dynamics often do so with different causal assumptions and different conclusions concerning the outcome. Models based on biological and environmental relationships vary from pessimism about the consequences of population growth to a qualified optimism based on a perception that in the long term population pressure has been the mainspring of technical, economic and social progress. This chapter outlines the determinants of popu-lation change and examines the major models which incorporate them into their explanation of historical change.

Some fundamental principles of demography can be stated simply. The number of births relative to deaths in a particular period determines the direction and rate of population change. Leaving aside the parameters of particular populations such as age and sex distribution, deaths depend on two sets of determinants. The first group is normal mortality associated with ageing, endemic disease and the normal hazards of life; the second consists of mortality peaks occasioned by social and natural disasters, notably war, famine and epidemic disease.

McNeill (1976) has drawn attention to epidemic disease as a cause of major downswings in population. The important relation-ships in McNeill's model are those between micro-organisms and their human hosts.[1] These relationships have been affected by changing population densities and the sporadic confluences of disease-pools that have resulted from the movements of conquerors and traders. The near-genocidal impact of diseases introduced into the Americas as a lethal (though unintended) part of the 'Columbian Exchange' (Crosby, 1972) are well known. Less spectacular but of great significance are the epidemics that afflicted Europe in the sixth, fourteenth and seventeenth centuries AD and began three population cycles or logistics (Cameron, 1989). These surges and declines in population totals were mirrored by those of China (McEvedy and Jones, 1978).

The other determinant of population change, the birth rate, depends on social factors like the age of marriage, proportion of the population married, the ratio of males to females, and social customs which reduce the effective birth rate below the biological maximum. Among these are duration of lactation and infanticide.

If the birth rate exceeds the death rate, population will increase; the question then arises whether additional provisions will be available to support the additional consumers. At the close of the eighteenth century Thomas Robert Malthus in his *Essay on the Principle of Population* (1798; Winch, 1987) addressed this problem and few discussions on demography since have been able to avoid referring to his model.

Malthus's model rests on two propositions: population can increase in geometric progression, e.g. 2, 4, 8, 16, 32 . . ., while the means of subsistence can be increased only arithmetically, e.g. 2, 3, 4, 5, 6 . . . He establishes the first of these propositions on the premise that the attraction between the sexes was unchanging, and on the belief that this attraction would allow the population to double in each generation. The second proposition rests on the tendency to diminishing returns that is to be found in a two-factor model of production when one factor (resources) remains relatively fixed while the other (labour) is increased, all other things constant.

The assumption of little growth in resources is crucial. Given the assumptions, the conclusion that scarcity of the means of subsistence would result from population increase is inescapable. Malthus asserted that positive and preventive checks would then raise the level of mortality or reduce the level of births so as to bring together the divergent trends of population and food supply. The principal positive checks were war, disease and famine; the preventive checks were associated with vice – defined to include contraception. 'All these checks may be fairly resolved into misery and vice' (Malthus, 1798: *103*).

With his short essay, Malthus converted the philosophic optimism of the eighteenth century into the pessimism of the nineteenth. Economics seemed less to do with 'the wealth of nations' about which Smith had written a generation earlier than with an inexorable poverty of nations. For many, the model provided a self-evident conclusion: any attempt to alleviate poverty would increase the sum of misery. Private or public charity would simply call forth a flood of pauper babies. This attitude influenced poor law legislation in England in the nineteenth century.

Criticism of the model nevertheless came at once. Critics pointed out that the birth rate is not a simple function of food supplies, but instead is dependent on social behaviour, which in turn is influenced by custom and expectations as well as by the current availability of subsistence. Malthus took the point. In the second edition of his *Essay*, he allowed for a new check which acted to reduce the birth rate. This was 'moral restraint': delayed marriage, celibacy and sexual abstinence. He, and most of his contemporaries, were confident that in practice this 'prudential' check would have little significance. Yet, the compelling logic of his model rested on its simple biological base and that was destroyed by the acknowledged possibility of prudential behaviour. The 'Malthusian trap' could be broken.

The Malthusian trap exists when any increase in income per head is swamped by an increase in population, the result being that income per head falls back to its previous subsistence level. If on the other hand the increase in income per head is sufficiently large, or is expected to persist for long enough, the population response need not negate its effects. With reproduction a matter of individual choice rather than instinct, having and rearing children becomes subject to a calculus of cost and benefit with respect to the number thought desirable. If affluence increases, the delights of family life may remain constant, but the economic benefit of children, principally their support for the family unit and for aged parents, becomes less important. Similarly, as wealth in a hitherto traditional society increases, the direct and indirect costs of children will increase: these are the costs of keeping and educating children and the cost of the opportunities foregone by a woman in devoting her time to them.

The other Malthusian proposition, that the means of subsistence could be increased only slowly, failed in two respects. Firstly, matters other than the specified variable population need not and did not remain constant. In the nineteenth century, technical and organizational change continually shifted the production function upward, increasing the possibility of increased output. Consequently, population and income per head in Europe moved together rather than inversely as required by the Malthusian model and as appears to have been the case over most of previous history. Secondly, Malthus assumed that population change and technical progress were independent variables, except that the pace of the latter indirectly constrained the former. However, others have postulated that population increase generates changes in both technology and organization. When population increases there may be more options available to people than Malthus allowed.

Ester Boserup (1965; 1981) has much more recently argued that both rural and urban production are increased in response to population pressure. In her model, the intensification of land use consequent upon increasing rural population takes the form of a transition from hunting and gathering to agriculture, first to shifting cultivation, then through short fallowing to annual cropping, finally to multi-cropping. Although output per hectare and total output increase, output per unit of labour effort falls: diminishing returns persist in this sense. Effort must be increased, with the abundant factor labour substituting for the scarce factor land. Population pressure (with a knowledge of agricultural techniques that can be used to increase output) leads to an irreversible change from a less to a more arduous way of providing food.

Population increase can also increase productivity by making feasible 'density-dependent' projects such as irrigation systems and transport facilities (Boserup, 1981). Roads, bridges, ports and railways reduce transport costs, which widens the market and induces increases in output through specialization in production. Improved transport also increases consumer satisfaction by making available a wider choice of commodities. However, such projects are feasible only if there is enough labour for their construction and sufficient (potential) density of traffic for their economic use. Given more people, the cost of constructing this infrastructure, or social overhead capital, bears lightly on each individual. The productivity gains are those of economies of scale. These are reductions in cost per unit product that occur when the scale of production expands, whether in a unit of production or in the economy generally, with all factors of production able to be varied in quantity. While Malthus's analysis rested on one factor being fixed and the other variable, in Boserup's model labour or fertilizers and machinery can be substituted for other resources enough to permit economies of scale.

A further way in which the pressure of population on resources may stimulate production is by the shift in income that would occur away from the peasantry to those who own or control the increasingly scarce resources, such as good soil, or land suitable for irrigation. This concentration of wealth, provided it is not squandered on conspicuous consumption, can be used to undertake investment in projects that may be productive but require 'lumpy' large amounts of capital.

The Boserup model can contribute an understanding of the rise and decline of some ancient civilizations in a way that Wittfogel's 'hydraulic civilization' model or the Marxist static 'Asiatic mode of production' cannot do. Boserup's cycle begins with population increase resulting in an increasing intensity of agricultural production, investment in infrastructure including transport, and the emergence of cities. Cities are density-dependent in terms of the extent to which the limited surplus of agricultural output per head above subsistence needs can be collected from the peasants and made available to urban dwellers. The volume collected depends on the number of peasants, their productivity and the transport system. If expansion continues, a point will be reached where the need for labour for current production, for construction and maintenance of capital works, and for the army cannot be met: economies of scale are not infinite. The result is eventual economic stagnation and military vulnerability.

Boserup perceives this cycle in the operation of irrigation-based societies of the Middle East and less dramatically in Europe. Intensified farming – short fallow and three-field rotation – accom-

panied population increase in Europe between the ninth and fourteenth centuries, but agricultural production was not infinitely
responsive to intensification. Increasing the area of the arable
meant lower average fertility through the use of less fertile land,
less fallowing and, as pastures were ploughed, less grazing for
animals that provided food, draught and dung. These changes led
to deforestation in Europe. China encountered similar problems,
with soil erosion added.

Population trends in China were strikingly similar in timing and
direction to those of Europe. This has been accounted for by the
spread of diseases (McNeill, 1976), and more tentatively by the
effects in the seventeenth century of the Little Ice Age (Parker and
Smith, 1978). However, the parallels with Europe in the early
modern period end with demography. After the efflorescence of
the Song dynasty, the Chinese economy showed little evidence of
development, that is, of sustained increase of income per capita
based on changing technical and/or institutional structures. To
explain this, Elvin (1973) offers an explanation that is essentially
Malthusian but also implicitly draws on the Boserup model.

Elvin argues that in China intensification of effort and minor but
virtually continuous improvement, especially in agriculture,
allowed total output to increase with population growth. This
process continued until it was halted by a lack of further opportunities to increase output, given pre-industrial methods. By the late
Qing dynasty, population pressed on resources but the large
absolute quantity of inputs that would have been needed made any
great leap into industrialization impossible.

The model provides a useful intellectual framework but Elvin's
dismissal of other factors traditionally offered in explanation of
China's stasis is not convincing. The structure of Chinese society
and polity, notably the power and conservatism of the bureaucracy
(Balazs, 1964) and the low status of merchants, were influential
too. Similarly, the land available for cultivation was not fixed
during the period. This eased the pressure of population and
reduced the need to innovate. Population increase was partly
accommodated by the Han people migrating into sparsely settled
areas in the south and west, and later into Manchuria (Jones,
1981).

Models based on demography offer explanations of why economic and social change followed population increase but seldom specify how individuals translate pressure on resources into social action. Colinvaux (1983) suggests a mechanism based on the principles of bioecology. His two essential assumptions are that human breeding strategy is such that in aggregate the number of offspring desired by families will be greater than is needed to replace the parents, and that in deciding on a number of children parents consider the cost of preparing them for a 'niche' or socially appropriate place in society. Hence, paradoxically the poor can 'afford' more children per family than can the rich. When population expands relative to resources the poor go hungry but upper classes are confronted with fewer opportunities for their offspring. They can and do act to create new 'niches'.

Colinvaux argues that these niches are opened by developing trade, settling colonies, by imperial conquests, and, less convincingly, by the development of new manufacturing methods. The analysis is consistent with European experience, and suggests why empires were sought and tenaciously held even when they appear in aggregate terms not to have been profitable: empires offered opportunities for military and civil careers to the children of the politically effective classes. In a similar way, the expansion of the Chinese people south and west from a heartland in the valley of the Huang He river offered not only land for young peasants but new administrative posts for the qualified offspring of the scholar-gentry.

The models discussed in this chapter are pessimistic about either the immediate or the long-term future of humanity, given continued population growth. In the Malthusian model a crisis is ever-threatening; in Boserup's the crisis is only long delayed.[2] Both took the view expressed by Colinvaux that 'we can defer the final poverty but not avoid it' (*p. 38*). However, technical change falsified Malthus's predictions. It has since been urged that continued economic progress can be based on technical change, despite or even because of population increase.

5
Deus ex machina? Technology and science

Technical change is a necessary element in the process of economic development. Capital goods, the produced means of production in which much of technical change has been embodied, have enormously increased production and reduced its cost in terms of labour, materials, time and risk. In the absence of technical change, the Smithian process of growth by capital accumulation and division of labour would eventually encounter diminishing returns; development is not simply a matter of increasing capital goods of the same type but of the provision of better or different capital goods. This capital deepening, necessary for continued productivity increase, is exemplified by the shift from pack-horse to horse-drawn wagons and through canal boat to steam trains. By contrast, capital widening is simply an increase in capital gained by reproducing the existing units, the prevailing methods.

The importance of technical change to material progress is obvious, so obvious that it appears in some models at least implicitly as a general explanation of economic and historical change. However, the thesis depends on technical change being an independent variable. A long-term perspective shows that not to have been the case. Technology is more appropriately seen as dependent on the institutional structure and the availability of capital, including 'human capital' expressed as an educated, skilled and healthy workforce.[1] The availability of capital is in turn dependent on a favourable set of institutions.

The weakness of explanations of historical change that rely on prior changes in technology is that they fail to demonstrate that technology was the cause rather than merely the instrument of change. The problem associated with explanatory models based on technical change as the causal variable is well illustrated by a simple example, a presentation in which the introduction of stirrups was said to have been responsible for feudalism.

Lynn White Jr (1962) argues that the feudal structure of the medieval period was the consequence of the introduction of the stirrup into Western Europe in the eighth century. Stirrups gave a rider sideways stability, matching the front and rear support afforded by a saddle's high pommel and cantle. Secured in this way, a mounted warrior could fight more effectively, being able in a charge to concentrate the momentum of horse and rider into the tip of his lance. So militarily decisive was this innovation, argues White, that the stirrup was immediately adopted, with the associated techniques and tactics of cavalry action. As usual in matters of defence, cost was a problem. Considerable resources were required to train, maintain and equip a single knight, and *a fortiori* a cavalry force. Europe in the eighth century had no system of taxation to meet defence needs. The solution was for a ruler to grant land and labour to individual warriors to support them as military specialists, in return for which they pledged loyalty. In White's view, the necessary consequence of the use of the stirrup was the creation of the feudal structure, with its code of chivalry (from *cheval*, a horse) and its manorial base.

Although elegant in its simplicity, this deterministic perception of the origins of feudalism has been criticized as misleading (Hilton and Sawyer, 1963). The military pre-eminence of the mounted knight on medieval battlefields did not depend on a technical innovation; the stirrup merely made what was a second-best defence system more effective.

Historically, infantry supported when possible by cavalry and missile troops has been the preferred military structure. The development and success of the Macedonian phalanx, Roman legion and Spanish *tercio* attest to this. But infantry is effective only in large, cohesive and disciplined formations. Effective infantry armies are very expensive to raise, train and maintain; they presuppose the existence of a populous, productive economy, with an effective taxation system. These requirements were met only in classical and again in modern times. As Roman revenues declined in the late Empire, reliance on infantry declined – mounted warriors increasingly bore the burden of an increasingly ineffective defence. A millennium later, productivity and administrative capacity grew with the development of nation-states and infantry once more became the core of armies. Between those times, in the Middle Ages, recourse was had to the knight as a cheaper form of defence. Knights with castles provided local protection and could be summoned, through the obligations of fealty to their liege lord, to form larger military formations.

The feudal array was definitely not an ideal solution to the problem of defence. Armoured knights were effective against raiders and rebellious peasants but were repeatedly defeated when matched against large bodies of trained and disciplined infantry, notably the Swiss, even though the infantry was armed with weapons no more advanced technically than bows and arrows or long spears called pikes.

Reversing the supposed direction of causation in the model gives better results. A model of change in military technology resulting from the economic circumstances of the early Middle Ages is more plausible than one in which military technology is the determining variable. Labour was relatively scarce, productivity low, transport was poor, obligations were met in services or goods, not cash. Defence could be provided only by military forces that were dispersed, drawing on the local community for maintenance while offering it protection. Tactical mobility and strategic concentration were permitted by putting the warriors on horseback. The stirrup simply made this necessary solution to the problems of local and regional defence more effective.

The thesis that technical change is primarily a product of economic need is supported by studies of the technology of ships. Certainly, in the pre-scientific era, innovation was discouraged by the hazardous environment in which ships operated: ill-conceived innovation in design or construction could well cost lives and capital. Yet changes did occur, at times rapidly, in response to changes in specific economic requirements (Unger, 1980). Also, there are cases of apparent technical reversion that prove the rule. As Europe sank into the Dark Ages, Mediterranean shipwrights adopted less skilled building techniques. This deterioration in the quality of ships was not because technology had been lost; it was a rational response to changes in the volume and nature of trade and in the relative cost of materials and labour. Ships were built by simpler, less labour-intensive techniques, with less metal but more of the relatively abundant wood being used (Unger, 1980: *42, 105*). The primary causes of improvement in marine design were economic factors, although there was a feedback effect: the diffusion of improved design increased the efficiency of sea-transport and through this affected the economy.

The issue of whether technology is an independent or dependent explanatory variable can be presented more clearly by separating technical change into invention and innovation. Invention may be defined as conceiving an idea for some change and demonstrating its feasibility. Innovation is the incorporation of an invention into the production process. A further useful distinction, to be discussed later, is one between science which deals with basic principles and technology which relates to the current state of technique.

There may be a random element in the process of invention but it is likely that the efforts of even the most eccentric inventor will be influenced, at least, by perceived need – by the scarcity of some factor of production, or by an increase in demand for some commodity. To the extent that inventors are concerned with public recognition or material rewards, invention will be reduced to the status of dependent variable.

Even if invention were a wholly random process, perceived need would determine which inventions among the many would be selected for use. Innovation, putting techniques into use, is by definition a response to demand. A new technique is introduced into the production process only if it serves some purpose, either to increase output of a desired good or service, or to reduce costs. In Boserup's model of innovation in agriculture, demand generated by pressure of population leads to the adoption of changes which increase food output. The model has been generalized to offer an explanation of technical change in other important activities, notably transport and manufacturing (Boserup, 1981; Simon, 1977; 1983). In these cases, increased population density provides the incentive for change as well as a larger pool of inventive people.[2] However, these explanations are in terms of the provision of incentives, and if the institutional structure or a lack of capital were to prevent the operation of these incentives then technical progress would be retarded or stifled.

In more recent times, the imperative for change has lain in the pressure not of population but on profits resulting from competition in the market. The direction as well as the rate of technical change is affected by a desire to increase or at least preserve profit levels. These ends are pursued by attempting to rectify an imbalance between related technical processes or by seeking ways to overcome an actual or anticipated scarcity of some factor of production (Rosenberg, 1976).

An often cited (and much debated) example of scarcity affecting technical progress in England is the substitution of coal as a fuel for the allegedly increasingly scarce wood. Another example of Rosenberg's 'inducement mechanisms and focusing devices' is the reactive process driven by the scarcities or bottlenecks that occurred at different stages of the process of production of cotton textiles during the British Industrial Revolution. In the eighteenth century, Kay's flying-shuttle increased weavers' demand for yarn, which was met by the development of machines for spinning cotton: Hargreaves' spinning jenny, the 'water frame' which utilized water power, and a machine incorporating features of both earlier inventions, the 'mule'. The cheaper yarn created a boom in hand-loom weaving, with a consequent incentive to invent and develop a power-driven loom. Technology thus both stimulates and responds to technical change. In military technology progress is often expressed as the result of a similar reactive process involving alternating improvements in weapons and means of defence.[3]

A further means of technical advance is the self-explanatory 'learning by doing' whereby experience in one operation leads to improvement in that and associated operations (David, 1975). Although this and other processes may seem to be wholly technical, the incentive behind them is not: 'at the secondary, entrepreneurial, level of technical change, economic motives must be regarded as primary' (Mokyr, 1985: 28).

Changes which reduce labour effort do not require for their introduction some form of compulsion, such as is imposed by population pressure. Population expansion follows rather than precedes that sort of change (Simon, 1977). Improved agricultural calendars, metal implements and firearms, for example, have been adopted readily by those cultures to which such elements of advanced technology have been introduced.

The speed and effectiveness of the adoption of technology have depended on two sets of factors. The first is the requirement of technical consistency, that is, whether the necessary associated products are available. Successful artillery, for example, depended on advances in metallurgy. So important is the requirement of technical consistency that the periods of most rapid technical progress were those in which there was a 'clustering' of inventions, as in the British Industrial Revolution.

The second set of factors influencing the speed of adoption of new technology is that pertaining to the culture of the society. The importance of culture can be illustrated by considering firearms. All societies were anxious to acquire these weapons but it was the Europeans who used them to greatest effect (Cipolla, 1970; Parry, 1981). The Ottoman Turks, warriors but not technicians, increasingly fell behind Europeans in the effectiveness of their artillery. Oriental states and empires possessed cannon, but lacked a technically able 'middle class' to provide soldiers who could efficiently use and maintain the guns (Parkinson, 1965: *202*). For different reasons, the Tokugawa Japanese gave up guns altogether. Aristocrats in Japan as elsewhere resented the social implications of the use of guns and in contrast to European aristocracies the Japanese did not consider them indispensable for defence against foreigners (Perrin, 1980). Moreover, firearms in private hands were a threat to the power of the central authority.

The technology of the modern world is science-based and nowadays the case for science as the propellant of technical change might seem overwhelming. Yet until recent times the direct contribution of science was limited. Even as late as the Industrial Revolution, changes in technology normally preceded scientific understanding of the principles on which they rested (Rosenberg, 1982: *144*). By contrast, the scientific *attitude* of observation, calculation and experiment had emerged in Europe during the Middle Ages, and developed with the Renaissance and the Scientific Revolution to provide in early modern times an intellectual climate of inquiry based on observation or experiment, and on calculation, classification and inference. Rostow (1975) argues that a decisive element in the post-medieval development of Europe was the indirect effect of progress in science.

However, as with technology, the acceptance of scientific inquiry was conditioned by the nature of society. Inquiry was at its most free in Protestant northern Europe, whereas it was restricted by the Counter-Reformation in the Catholic south, suppressed in the Ottoman empire and neglected in late Imperial China. Indeed, the scientific and technical stasis that followed the remarkable achievements of the Song dynasty, or the flowering of early Islam, indicates that scientific inquiry and technology do not necessarily possess in themselves the dynamism suggested by the European experience.

Marx's schema, based on the European experience, may appear in a simple reading to depend upon technical determinism: 'the handmill gives you society with the feudal lord; the steam-mill, society with the industrial capitalist'. But the Marxist model is really more subtle (Rosenberg, 1982: *36*). In it, technology interacts with the dialectical process occurring in the social structure: technical change breeds stresses within society that culminate in political revolution, which allows further technical change. Marx argues that the Industrial Revolution followed from the overthrow of the feudal aristocracy and the establishment of capitalist (bourgeois) control.

While the primacy of technology is useful as a heuristic device, it is misleading as an explanation of long-term change. Beneath technical change in the causal sequence lies the social and institutional structure (Rosenberg, 1976). A structure which permits competition in the civil or military spheres will encourage innovation, as did the nation-state system of Europe. The Europeans refined their techniques of conquest in intra-European conflicts, and developed their commercial and manufacturing skills in the context of mercantilist competitiveness. The reasons for invention and innovation, rather than the techniques or machines themselves, are the crucial considerations in explaining long-term change. These lie more in the institutions that guide human activity.

6
Institutions and change: theory and history

I

The themes that are the centrepieces of the models already out-lined have been incorporated by Douglass North with R. P. Thomas into an 'institutional' explanation of long-term changes in the structure and performance of economic systems (North and Thomas, 1970; 1973; North, 1981). North broadly defines institutions as 'the forms of co-operation and competition that human beings develop and the systems of enforcement of these rules of organizing human activity'. He places them at the heart of economic history (1981: *17*). Institutions may be fundamental, as is a constitution specifying property rights, or they may be secondary, such as forms of financial institutions or rules of etiquette.

The importance of institutions in the process of change lies in whether they provide incentives for individuals to engage in productive activities: production itself, investment, invention and innovation. The value of these activities to society is obviously high. To the extent that institutions bring the private benefit of engaging in them closer to the public benefit of doing so, the activities will be encouraged and economic development will occur.

In the North and Thomas model, the driving force is the interaction of population change with resources, the supply of resources being in a Malthusian way relatively unresponsive to the changes in demand that population change causes. Population growth therefore encounters diminishing returns in agriculture, which alters the relative scarcity of labour and land and hence their prices. This in turn causes disequilibrium and change in the institutional structure. The process is held to account for the increasing privatization of productive resources during the Middle Ages.

In considering the early modern period, North and Thomas refocus attention to explain the implications of choices in a struggle, not directly for resources, but for tax revenues in the emergent nation-states. Choice is always constrained by economic frictions called transaction costs – the costs of search, negotiation and enforcement. The conclusion of the analysis is that failure to realize the productive potential inherent in a given state of knowledge may be ascribed to an inappropriate institutional structure. This closely resembles the essence of Marxist analysis; indeed, the shadow of Marx from time to time falls across this consciously non-Marxist model.

North shares with Marx a concern to incorporate into a model elements crucial to change in history – technology, population, and interest groups – which are neglected in the abstract, frictionless and static theoretical formulations based on neoclassical economics. In contrast to Marx, technical change is generally seen in North's analysis as a dependent and not an independent variable, being a function of the degree to which incentive to invest, invent and innovate is generated by the institutional structure. Technical knowledge is at most a necessary condition for increasing productivity. Although the sum of technical knowledge has been largely cumulative, economic progress has not. Accordingly, institutional constraints on the application of that knowledge rather than the technology itself are the appropriate area for any study which aims to elucidate the reasons for economic development, stagnation or decline.

The crucial behavioural assumptions in North's model (1981) are self-interest and economic rationality: individuals will endeavour to maximize their welfare, generally by seeking to maximize their income and wealth. This implies that individuals have stable preferences relating to wealth, leisure and risk; that as resources are finite, choices must be made; and that other things being equal individuals will prefer more goods and services to fewer (*p. 4*). The wealth-maximizing assumption is justified on the grounds that although no individual may exercise choice in those terms – and strictly speaking, none can in a world of uncertainty (*p. 6*) – scarcity and consequent competition in the market or otherwise will ensure an outcome as if they had. Those who make choices which are rational in the above respects have a higher probability of survival.

In terms of this individualistic calculus, simple aggregation is an obvious way of dealing with the actions of large groups, the members of which share a 'commonality of interest' (*p. 61*). The approach is comparable with but more flexible than the Marxist use of classes. However, analysis of group behaviour based on self-interest fails to explain inertia and change adequately when these conflict with the interests of the group. To explain inertia, why large groups fail to alter circumstances not in their members' interests, a consideration of the 'free-rider' problem is necessary. A free rider is a third party who enjoys the benefit of a transaction without contributing to its cost: 'rational individuals will not incur the costs of participating in large group action when the individual benefits can still be received by being a free rider' (*p. 10*). As it would seem to be in no individual's interest to act in those circumstances, the group remains passive. The free-rider problem also explains why change is usually imposed from near the apex of the political structure or by small elite groups (*p. 32*). The smaller the group, the less likely there is to be a 'free-rider' problem.

The calculus of self-interest also fails to explain action which does not appear to offer individual material benefits that are commensurate with expected cost. Altruism, or self-sacrifice in the furthering of some political or religious cause, are obvious examples of such behaviour. To explain this, a theory of ideology is necessary. This is not provided by North, although he does discuss the problem in the context of the model.

If the individualistic calculus were rigorously followed, the social system would be a jungle of ruthless and destructive competitiveness; the costs of enforcing rules of behaviour would be prohibitively high. An ideology which impels individuals to abide by a set of rules that may not be to their immediate benefit is a necessary condition for social stability in that it legitimizes existing institutions. To be acceptable, an ideology must depend on a belief that the existing rules are fair. Religious instruction is ideological as is much of military training and, less obviously, the influence of family and school. By contrast, one traditional purpose of a university is to induce healthy questioning of currently-held assumptions. Perhaps this is a reason why some governments have been ambivalent in their attitudes towards universities.

Resting as it does on moral judgement, ideology is not amenable to analysis by the techniques of economics. In the model, ideology is largely an independent variable, formed broadly by geography and developed by occupation, but North suggests an interesting dependent aspect, *viz.* the greater the occupational specialization in society, the greater the cost of devising moral codes (*p. 56*). Members of small groups who share common interests can more readily subscribe to a morality that limits free-riding than can members of fragmented societies. North uses this hypothesis in his account of the ideological turmoil of the last century when Western societies changed so fast. The concept would seem equally relevant to the religious turmoil in early modern Europe.

The core of explanation in this model is the extent to which institutions are efficient, that is to say, the extent to which property rights are defined and enforced so as to bring the net private benefit and the net social benefit of an activity closer to equality. Institutions efficient in this sense provided incentive for individuals who, reaping the full benefit of their activities, strove to increase their productivity. Explaining the ways in which efficient or inefficient institutions have developed at various places over time is the task of the analysis within the model. Before proceeding to examine the application to European history, it will be useful to consider the nature of the key concepts in more detail.

Institutions are collections of rules ordering the ways in which individuals and groups co-operate and compete. They may be specified in the forms of statute and regulation, embodied in formal organisations ranging from government to firms or families, or simply the ways of custom. Institutions foster economic growth – defined minimally as sustained increase in output – if they tend to bring the private rate of return on economic activity closer to the social rate. Equality of these rates is the ideal (and assumption) in pure economic theory. The discovery of improved techniques of production has a high value to a society, but the institutional structure has often not been such as to reward discoverers by allowing them to reap benefits commensurate with the costs incurred. To meet this institutional deficiency, rewards have been offered for the solution of particular technical problems such as the development of a marine chronometer. To encourage inventive activity on a wide front a patent system is more effective.

The incentive that an efficient institution can generate extends beyond inducements to engage more actively in invention or in current production. The institutional structure influences saving and investment and thus affects future output. In despotic or chaotic regimes the arbitrariness and consequent insecurity of property offers little or no incentive to save and accumulate productive assets; visible wealth invites confiscation or theft (Jones, 1988).

In the model, clearly specified and effectively enforced property rights are central to economic progress. Property rights refer to entitlements associated with property and it is these rights that are really being negotiated when property is bought and sold. The more precisely the property is specified and the rights over it defined, the less will be the costs of negotiation, one of the 'transaction costs'. Other transaction costs relating to the transfer of rights between principals are those of search, information, and enforcement of contract. Negotiation and enforcement costs can be reduced by the existence and authority of a body of law. Search and information costs can be reduced by growth of the market because there are economies of scale in the collection and dissemination of information. Reduced transaction costs permit more of the benefits of exchange to accrue to the principals in the transaction: trade may therefore be expected to increase and with it specialization and productivity.

The importance of specified and enforced property rights is illustrated by contrasting the utilization of an open-access resource with a resource over which defined and exclusive property rights exist. In the case of the ocean fisheries, for example, it is in the interest of each individual fisherman to fish as intensively as possible, even though this may totally deplete the resource. With each individual acting in his or her own interest, unrestrained by any property rights other than possession, it is to each person's advantage to maximize his or her catch. This may be true even when as individuals they are aware of the consequences of their actions and would prefer a different result.

The ocean fisheries problem can be overcome by collective action to allocate property rights in terms of gear, quotas, fishing zones or time on the fishing ground. As it would be to each individual's advantage to break the arrangement, these rights must be enforced. In this, as in most other institutional arrangements, enforcement is most effective and its costs are lowest if the task is undertaken by the state: naval, coastguard or fisheries patrols in territorial waters are a recognition of this. A fish farm would have no comparable problems. On the contrary, the associated sharply defined and easily enforced property rights would be an inducement to increase productivity.

The steps from open access resource through communal property to individual property rights will provide increased incentive and allow the managerial flexibility necessary to increase productivity. However, historically the story does not end there as it might in pure economic theory. For development it is not simply exclusive property rights but who holds those rights that is important. Because of this, and to consider the distribution of wealth and income, North goes on to examine the nature and functioning of the state.

A widely criticized gap in North's early work was the lack of a theory of the state, the neglect of political forces that form the core of alternative, Marxist interpretations of history (Brenner, 1985). North subsequently formulated a theory of the state, based on economic analysis, but one in which the function of the state was narrow: it served the interests of those who controlled it. Accordingly, the model can incorporate manifestations of what Marxists would term 'the class struggle'.

The primary purpose of the state has been to provide defence and order in return for revenue. The state is 'an organization with a comparative advantage in violence, extending over a geographic area whose boundaries are determined by its power to tax constituents' (North 1981: *21*). There are economies of scale in the provision of protection – it can be provided most cheaply by a single producer (Lane, 1958). Since distance, organizational problems, and physical or cultural boundaries will increase the cost of defence, there is an optimum size of state for each level of military technology and organizational skill. The state specifies the property right structure, the rules of possession and exchange, and it enforces compliance (North, 1984). In this model North sees the state as being essentially but not wholly predatory. The property rights specified by the state are those which are most favourable to the ruler's interests. Within that structure the state then endeavours to reduce transaction costs. A universal example of this is the establishment of uniform weights and measures: uniformity favoured economic growth but its primary purpose was to facilitate tax collection (North, 1981: *43*).

The state, or ruler embodying the state, seldom enjoys a secure monopoly position. There is always at least potential competition from ambitious subjects or neighbours. The extent to which revenue can be extracted from subjects depends on the alternative sources of protection available to them. Accordingly, property rights have often been granted on political criteria – those with greatest wealth and power escaping the heavier impositions. For comparable reasons, property rights have been granted on the criteria of ease of collection of resultant revenue. This effectively minimizes the cost borne by the state but as in the case of a grant of monopoly it is likely to inhibit growth. In sum, the provision of property rights by the state is a necessary condition for economic growth, yet because of political motives it has been a sufficient condition only where the state has been to a significant degree the instrument of those people who stood to gain most from development. The Dutch Republic in the seventeenth century, the United States in the eighteenth century, and Britain in the nineteenth century are cases in point.

II

North (1981) uses the concepts outlined above to account for changes fundamental in the long-term course of European history – the Neolithic Revolution, the rise and decay of feudalism, and the Industrial Revolution. Moreover, the analysis in the model illuminates the reasons for the differential economic performance of nation-states in early modern Europe and by extension the different performance of European and other economic systems. The strengths and weaknesses of the model are illustrated in these applications.

The Neolithic Revolution, the transition from hunting and gathering to settled agriculture which occurred about 10,000 years ago, can be analysed in terms of the relationship between a growing population and a relatively fixed resource of wild animals. When game became scarce relative to the demand for it and productivity in hunting fell, groups turned to the cultivation of wild grasses. North argues that wild animals are an open-access resource and therefore overexploited, whereas agricultural production lends itself to the establishment of exclusive property rights, with incentives to develop practices that improve productivity. Also, a uniform progress in human technical ability would favour agriculture in the long term: any improvement in agricultural technology would offer a rise in yield, while improvements in hunting technology would accelerate the depletion of game stocks.

Scholars have often discussed the improvements in productivity brought by the Neolithic Revolution: the novelty of North's approach is that it highlights a revolution in incentives to increase production which was occasioned by the growing scarcity of traditional food sources. This insight does not rest on the widely criticized assumption that prior to agriculture, feral animals were an open-access resource, available to any hunter. If as a result of scarcity a group of hunter-gatherers established control over a territory, then that establishment by the group of an exclusive communal property in the animals *and* plants in the defended area would have provided an incentive for conservation. A necessary step would have been the domestication of plants.

The increase in productivity brought by settled agriculture was the foundation of the state, a development which North claims to have been the 'most fundamental achievement of the ancient world' (North, 1981: 94). Only the state could impose the structure of property rights that would enable an increasingly complex, partly urbanized society – a civilization – to function. The analysis of this functioning cannot, nevertheless, be solely economic. Necessary further elements were the opportunities of military technology, the accidents of geography, the legitimizing effects of ideology, and the contingent elements of human personalities.

Perhaps for these reasons, the institutional model leaves many of the crucial changes in the ancient world still to be explained: the extraordinary, indeed unique achievements of the Hellenic city-states or the conquests of Alexander, for example, or the domination of the Mediterranean basin by Rome, originally just one of many city-states in the region. However, the model does illuminate major aspects of change in that period. For instance, with the stabilization of the imperial frontiers, war ceased to be a profitable activity for the Romans. With the army no longer paid for by its conquests, taxes that had to be levied largely for military purposes increased to the point of alienating the most powerful citizens. These could establish a degree of political and fiscal independence on their estates, further depriving the Empire of revenue and accelerating the decline of trade. Meanwhile, the benefits of empire decreased. The central authority could no longer defend the frontiers or trade routes; its deployment of mobile forces defended only its ability to collect revenue. The Roman empire in the west ceased to exist as a coherent economic or political entity.

Serfdom, its nature and demise, and the feudal system erected upon it, is also explained within the framework of the model. The analysis is conducted largely in terms of the effect of population change on the institutional structure of the two most important economic sectors of the time, agriculture and commerce. Population change altered the relative scarcities of the factors land and labour, and by stimulating trade effected reductions in transaction costs.

Feudalism developed in the turbulence of late Dark Age Europe, when land was abundant relative to labour but was of value only if it was protected. Knights provided protection to peasants in return for their labour: a protection afforded whether particular peasants happened to want to be protected or not! Serfdom was the outcome, the relationship between lord and serf being one of coercion more than of contract, as the latter term is commonly understood (North, 1981: *130*; cf. North and Thomas, 1973: *32*). Labour dues, a characteristic of the early manorial system, may have been more appropriate than payments in goods given the high transaction costs (of negotiation) involved if the lord wished to vary the mix of commodities he consumed from those which were customarily available.

The model explains how population growth gave greater opportunities for specialization and trade. With trade came an increase in the quantity and variety of commodities available. Specialization of production was based on local resource endowments and factor proportions, that is not only on the nature of resources, but also on their relative scarcities. In the latter sense, abundance of land relative to labour determined the types of products that would be most profitable to produce. The increase in trade fostered the development of financial and commercial institutions, instruments and techniques which reduced transaction costs and further stimulated trade. In return for revenue the agrarian lords, serving their interest as petty rulers, provided protection for merchants and later granted them freedom within the merchants' creations, the towns. This reduction of risk encouraged capital accumulation and productive activity.

Population change, by altering relative factor scarcities, also destabilized the customary and stultifying service relationship of feudalism and the manor, ultimately replacing it with the more flexible cash nexus. With population growth, labour became relatively abundant and land scarce. The lords endeavoured to obtain exclusive property rights in land, while allowing serfs to commute their dues as the knights had commuted their military service obligations. In the century following the Black Death the population declined, and the model would predict that with the old relative factor scarcities re-established, those with power would try to bring back the old manorial obligations. This was indeed attempted in Western Europe, but unsuccessfully.

The explanation of this requires specification of power relationships. Each lord was more concerned to have his fields tilled than to collaborate with his peers in the attempt to reimpose the obligations of serfdom on peasants. A tenant farmer, on whatever terms, is better for the land than none: peasants were granted long leases at minimal rents. The lords thus failed to collude against the peasants – they fell victim to the free-rider problem as each furthered his own interest in seeking tenants.

By early modern times the land had been freed from feudal but not customary tenure with long, heritable leases. The next step in freeing the land came, predictably, with the rise in population in the sixteenth century. Again, with an increasing demand for food and wool, land became relatively scarce and the lords sought more exclusive property rights in it. In England, whence many of the data supporting the model are derived, their purpose was achieved by negotiation, legal and extra-legal action (Davis, 1973). The land they acquired was let out on short leases to tenants selected for their ability and (working) capital resources. The land was worked by landless labour. The tenurial structure provided incentives at all levels and was flexible, productive and market-oriented.

However, the establishment of exclusive property rights is not the end of the matter as North's work might suggest. Different forms of land tenure were established in different areas of Europe, with differing implications for productivity and growth (de Vries, 1976; Miskimin, 1977). Following Boserup (1964), the tenurial system may be classified into the categories of landlord and tenant, noble and serf, peasant proprietor, and sharefarmer. The advantages of the landlord and tenant system have been sketched above. By contrast, although production may have been efficient on estates in Eastern Europe owned by nobles and worked by serfs, the associated pattern of consumption was not such as to stimulate manufacturing or service industries in the region. In other parts of Europe where peasant proprietorship was common, development was retarded by peasants' lack of entrepreneurial ability, limited access to capital, and insulation from market pressures as well as by the burden of taxation. The sharefarming characteristic of the Mediterranean region was likewise conservative and undercapitalized.

The systems of tenure themselves reflected the differing power relationships that were established within the different states. The interest of the absolutist kings of France and nearby areas lay in supporting a tax-paying peasantry against the largely tax-exempt aristocracy, while in England the great lords, subjects of a more limited monarchy, acquired most of the land. In Eastern Europe and Russia, the peasants had less opportunity to evade lordly power, and the powerful nobility colluded with or against the state to impose on the peasantry an increasingly onerous serfdom. Although North does not examine these various situations, they are consistent with his analysis of the 'free-rider' problem and the 'constrained predator' state.

Briefly, in the 'constrained predator' model of the state, rulers with subjects who have recourse to alternative sources of protection and justice must bargain for revenue, typically offering property rights, directly or in the form of public goods and services (Jones,

1981). Similarly, an absence of a perceived need for protection strengthened the bargaining position of subjects. The need for protection was in turn related to their vulnerability to armed aggression, which was often a matter of geography. Britain, for example, being an island, was relatively secure from invasion. In such a situation, revenue for the king's military purposes could only be obtained by bargaining. This is illustrated by developments from Edward I's parliaments, to Charles I's 'ship money' crisis and his execution. The conflict was resolved when the Glorious Revolution of 1688 increased the power of parliament to match that of the king, so increasing the security of property rights (North and Weingast, 1989).

The waterlogged Netherlands was similarly defensible. Its location had helped to make it the *entrepôt* for northern Europe, a great centre of trade, manufacturing and commercial agriculture. Enough revenue had been forthcoming to induce a succession of overlords to allow the Low Countries to retain their economically efficient structure of property rights. When Philip II of Spain insisted on religious, fiscal and administrative uniformity within his empire, the Dutch rebelled, and prospered, while the financial and then the military power of Spain was broken.

Both England and the Netherlands passed through the 'General Crisis of the Seventeenth Century' little scathed, relative to the experience of France and Spain. In the latter countries, disorder and military exigencies had led the 'representative' assemblies to surrender their power to tax to absolutist monarchs. Following their perceived self-interest, these rulers altered property rights to favour the short-run collection of revenues – to the detriment of productivity and the potential for economic growth.

In his perspective of the Industrial Revolution, North rejects the traditional emphasis on technology. He argues that the Industrial Revolution, itself the expression of previous institutional change, was at core a change in the institutional structure. Increasing demands on manufacturing industry could be met, but only with increasing transaction costs as the market widened and division of labour intensified. To reduce these costs a new organisation of production was increasingly adopted – the factory system. In addition, improvement in the definition and enforcement of property rights raised returns to invention and innovation (North,

1981: *159ff*). The productive potential of the structure of institutions termed the capitalist system was overwhelmingly evident by the mid-nineteenth century. Marx, no friend to capitalists, wrote a striking tribute:

> The bourgeoisie, during its rule of scarce one hundred years, has created more massive and more colossal productive forces than have all preceding generations together . . . what earlier century had even a presentiment that such productive forces slumbered in the lap of social labour? (Marx and Engels, 1848: *85*)

With the eventual harnessing of science to production, the bourgeoisie went on to achieve still greater feats of productivity.

The institutional model provides a coherent, consistent and, at the level of generality for which it is designed, comprehensive framework within which the structure and performance of economies through time can be analysed. The model does not in itself represent a complete theory of historical change (North, 1981: *68*). The problem is not that theory originally developed to analyse markets cannot be applied to historical situations in which price-making markets of the nineteenth-century kind did not exist – as was urged by Polanyi (1944; North, 1977). Market activity appears to have been much more widespread than was once thought (Silver, 1983; Curtin, 1984); and in any case, economic analysis is essentially the calculus of choice, historical circumstances providing the content and constraints within which it must work. A challenge to the philosophical basis of the model (Field, 1981) has itself been shown to be flawed (Basu *et al.*, 1987). The real problem lies in the influences on change or stasis that are contingent or remain largely or wholly outside the model.

Within the model, the nature of property rights, particularly those related to the land, commerce and public revenue, determines economic performance. The structure of property rights was established as an outcome of the struggle for control within the nascent nation-states during the long early modern period *c.*1450 to *c.*1750 AD. To the extent that the outcomes depended on the personalities involved or on geographical factors they are not determined within the model. The model does not deal well with the Chinese experience wherein occurred changes in population levels comparable in timing and magnitude to those in Europe but with different effects. Much of the stuff of political and military history is also excluded from North's explanation.

Some apparently non-economic influences on behaviour could be brought within the scope of the model, at least partly. Geography, or more specifically location and resource endowment, can be specified in terms of relative cost structures, and much of military technique can be endogenized as indicated in chapter 5. A more intractable problem is the effect of ideology but in so far as the religion in a state was that of the ruler, its political consequences can be analysed in terms of the 'predator state'. The spread of and checks to the Reformation, for example, have a strong political element. The unpredictable actions of powerful individuals remain entirely outside the model (and also outside other models). Statisticians would refer to this as the error term in their equations; historians would make reference to Cleopatra's nose.

Doubts about the value of the model are not always based on the problems outlined, or even on a rejection of its fundamental assumptions, those of self-interest and economic rationality. One alternative model is itself based on self-interest, but an interest expressed in terms of political and market power. In this model, to be considered next, relationships were (and are) exploitative, rather than mutually beneficial as they are in conventional economic theory.

7
Development as exploitation?

Most economic models of economic development explain the process through the operation of one or a few key economic variables, the inference being that stagnation is to be explained by an absence of change in those variables. However, some scholars investigating the wide disparities of wealth between Europe and other areas of the modern world have constructed models in which both poverty and economic progress are explained by a single cause: the nature of exploitation inherent in the capitalist system. The argument of these models is that the structure of private ownership, market competition and state support that defines capitalism enabled the Europeans to exploit others, simultaneously enriching themselves and impoverishing societies elsewhere.

The exploitation that those models envisage as an integral part of the spread of capitalism arises from a relationship between regions. The 'core' region consists of states that are characterized by political unity, military power and advanced technology. The 'periphery' is a region of weak political units, inferior in technology. In this perspective, the periphery does not benefit from a dissemination of technology from the core, as both Marxist and liberal economists would expect. Nor does it benefit from specialization in production and associated trade as Adam Smith would have expected. Instead, the model specifies social and economic structures, set in place by the interaction between core and periphery, which actively condemn the latter to technical inferiority, political subservience and economic backwardness. Development in one area is necessarily accompanied by underdevelopment in the other: 'economic development and underdevelopment are opposite faces of the same coin' (Frank, 1967: 9).

Immanuel Wallerstein, with formidable scholarship, has provided the most historically comprehensive version of this model (Wallerstein, 1974a, b; 1980).

Wallerstein's analysis is based on the concept of a 'world-system'. 'World' in this context is used in a rhetorical way; it does not imply 'global', and may refer to a limited geographical area. A 'world-system' is a social system embracing multiple cultures, and is defined by a division of labour which makes its members economically interdependent (Wallerstein, 1974b: *390*). The system provides for the needs of individuals within it, but a limited exchange in luxury items may take place with those outside.

Of the two significant forms of world-system, one is a 'world-empire', its boundary being the limit of political control and its structure resting on a flow of tribute to the central authority. The other form of world-system is a 'world-economy', which is defined by specialization in production and market exchange. The 'surplus' production, that is, that above some loosely defined subsistence consumption level, still flows to the core of the system but as profit rather than tribute *per se*. Nevertheless, the flows are affected by the exercise of non-economic power at the local and systemic levels. Wallerstein's capitalist world-system is a world-economy of the type described. Emerging in the sixteenth century, it was unlike earlier world-economies in that it neither disintegrated nor was absorbed into the redistributive, bureaucratic structure of a single political empire. A powerful Habsburg emperor failed in the attempt: 'the failure of Charles V was the success of Europe' (Wallerstein, 1972: *95*). The early modern empires of England, France, Spain and Portugal are dismissed by Wallerstein as being merely 'nation-states with colonial appendages operating within the framework of a world-economy' (1974b: *391*).

The polities encompassed by the capitalist world-system fall into the categories of core, semi-periphery and periphery. These categories are notionally functional but in practice geographical. This ambiguity of the classificatory criteria is a weakness in the logical structure of the model.

Core, semi-periphery and periphery are analytically identified by the power of the state, the nature of specialization and the way in which labour is organized – or controlled. In the periphery, unfree labour – peons, serfs, slaves – produces raw materials and foodstuffs for the core areas, while in the core, free wage labour produces specialized agricultural products and manufactured goods, and provides commercial services. The production patterns determined initially by the comparative advantage of each area shape the various forms of control by which labour is exploited at the local level. Extensive monoculture, whether of grain on estates in Eastern Europe or of tropical products on plantations in the Americas, lends itself to cultivation by unfree labour: the level of skill required is low, supervision is easy, compulsion is effective. By contrast, mixed commercial farming and manufacturing involve complex processes and innovative activity. In those situations, a wage system with its flexibility and incentive structure is the more cost-efficient, and perhaps the only means of eliciting appropriate effort.

At the system-wide level, exploitation occurs as the definitionally powerful core states acquire commodities, 'surplus economic value' from the periphery, by a process of 'unequal exchange' (Wallerstein, 1974b: *401*). This process rests upon there being high wages in the core and low 'wages' (of some form) in the periphery. In that circumstance, it is argued, goods traded from the core would be expensive, and those from the periphery cheap, even though they may well have required the same quantity of labour in their production. The hypothesis rests for its plausibility upon 'wages' being determined in the periphery by non-economic forces: the power of the core to coerce the periphery, or within the periphery for the landowner to coerce the peasants. This explanation for the terms on which exchange took place begs questions about labour productivity and the supply of and demand for products.

The ability of core states to appropriate and accumulate 'surplus economic value' from the periphery arose also from monopolistic and monopsonistic trading positions, that is, trade in which there is one seller or one buyer. These positions were supported by legal sanctions and backed by naval power. In this, the model reflects the historical reality of the early modern period, when trade and warfare were characteristically conjoined. The political cohesion and military superiority of the core states gave them the opportunity to pursue their economic interests by non-economic means, to the disadvantage of the less powerful and less cohesive societies on the periphery.

It was clearly in the interests of those in the core states to maintain the pattern of specialization on which they perceived their wealth and power to rest. An example is the passage of the British Navigation Acts in the seventeenth century. These aimed to reserve for the home country manufacturing industry with its associated benefits, whilst obliging the colonies to concentrate on primary production. In so far as such attempts were successful, there would have been little scope in the periphery to diversify output or increase productivity beyond what was possible within the established pattern of production. The attitude of the land-owning elite in the periphery further consolidated the pattern of production and weakened the political structure. As exporters, the landowners had a vested interest in maintaining the pattern of production and trade, which at once profited them and weakened the local manufacturers who were their potential rivals.

The semi-periphery in Wallerstein's system is not, as might be expected from Frank's similar model (Frank, 1967), a link in a chain of exploitation between the periphery and the core. Rather, semi-periphery areas stand outside that process. They are exploited by the centre and themselves exploit the periphery, but they primarily fulfil the functions of a middle class within a state. They provide luxuries and services and, most importantly, they soften the dichotomy between exploiters and exploited, so helping to preserve the political stability of the system.

In Wallerstein's interpretation of history, the core of the European world economy was established in the 'long sixteenth century', that is, 1450 to 1640 AD. There has been earlier world-economies in Europe, around the Mediterranean and one based on Flanders, but these had been transient. In contrast, the European world-economy that emerged as the 'capitalist world-system' was based on Dutch energy, expertise, location and luck, and then more enduringly on French and English power.

In early modern Europe, agriculture was the dominant activity, and it was in this sector of the economy that Wallerstein finds the structure of the capitalist world system first evident. The emergence of the system was signalled by widespread production for the market in expectation of profit (Wallerstein, 1974b: 399). As the system developed, Eastern Europe was committed to large-scale monoculture and thus to peripheralization and relative stagnation: north-western Europe became the dynamic core.

With the expansion of the bounds of European control and influence, the pattern of core and periphery was established on a larger scale and over a wider area, notably in the New World. By the end of the nineteenth century, the capitalist world-system had become global in scope. Industrialization had demanded increased supplies of raw materials and wider markets, and it had supplied the military and transport technology to give effect to that demand. Areas approximating to the cores of earlier, more circumscribed world economies – in the Mediterranean for example – sank to semi-peripheral status, exporting luxuries and providing services, 'deindustrialized and agrarianized' (Wallerstein, 1972: 99).

The model is valuable in that it directs attention to economically integrated and politically connected systems as wholes, rather than simply to the separate polities that are their parts. Analysis focused on the political unit may be valid for some purposes, as economic activity is affected by legal systems and these are conterminous with political entities. It is also convenient to study political units because statistical data are generally collected for administrative areas. However, state boundaries do not delimit economic activity. For this reason, formal regions defined by political boundaries are likely to be of less interest to students of long-term change than functional regions over which the important economic processes operate (Pollard, 1981).

Another useful aspect of Wallerstein's approach is that it corrects perceptions of history in which the market system, or trade, is assumed to be free from manipulation and is necessarily – indeed definitionally – of benefit to all participants. Certainly, specialization increases productivity and in the absence of coercion parties will trade only if each believes it to be in his or her interest to do so. However, market power – monopoly or monopsony – or political power can affect the terms on which trade is undertaken. Moreover, patterns of resource ownership can result in trade benefiting only a relative few at the expense of the rest of those involved in the production process. Trade in commodities produced by slave labour and the slave trade itself are obvious examples.

A third merit of the model is that it emphasizes 'path dependency', the principle that options available in any period depend on events in previous periods (David, 1986). Demonstrating the degree of path dependency is a necessary task in any history. Once an individual or group takes a particular direction in production it may be costly to switch to another. Time and resources are necessary to reorient labour to new forms of production and the returns will be uncertain. Apart from this, established interests both within and beyond the area of production may use economic or political power to make any change more costly still. The world is not negotiated anew each instant as frictionless neoclassical economic analysis might imply, and the Wallersteinian formulation emphasizes this point.

Doubts have been expressed about the empirical validity of Wallerstein's model. While it may be agreed that in the sixteenth century there were networks of regional and inter-regional trade, the question is whether these amounted to an integrated world-system. Critics argue that they did not (e.g. Dodgshon, 1977). Even within Europe in the sixteenth century, specialization by functional area was limited; Britain, for example, was for long a net exporter of grain and imported quantities of manufactured goods. Further, much of the domestic industry in Northwestern Europe was stimulated by population pressure rather than by an emerging international division of labour.

More generally, a modern world-system is argued to be clearly discernible only in the nineteenth century when the transport of bulk commodities became cheap, manufacturing industry became sufficiently advanced to dominate extensive markets and sources of raw materials, and price-forming markets became sufficiently developed and integrated to result in a global division of labour (Mathias, 1986). Wallerstein himself accepts that in the sixteenth century the world-system was 'vast but weak'. However, the criticisms outlined do not defeat Wallerstein's purpose in so far as it is to trace the evolution of the modern world-system.

The fundamental weakness of the model is that it is descriptive rather than conclusive (Brewer, 1980: *167, 181*). For example, the core area of the European world-economy gained its status for-tuitously 'by a series of accidents – historical, ecological, geo-graphic' (Wallerstein, 1974b: *400*). More significantly, core states could be and were relegated to semi-peripheral status, and the reverse movements could and did occur – all in a way that could not be determined from the model. It might be expected that core states, enjoying technological superiority, political cohesiveness and capital accumulation, would be able to maintain their dominance indefinitely. However, skills and technology can be transferred to or developed within the periphery, which by definition has cheap labour and probably untapped natural resources. The transition of British North America to core status from the semi-periphery and of Japan from the area 'external' to the world-system are striking examples of the mobility of states. The emergence of new centres of economic power was matched by the semi-peripheralization or peripheralization of others. The ability of a core state to exploit the periphery seems not to have been as persistent as the model requires.

Further, the model does not stand up well to a quantitative test of one of its fundamental hypotheses. An examination of the exchange relationship between core and periphery offers little support for the thesis that European development was entirely or even largely the consequence of exploitation of less well organized regions (O'Brien, 1982).

To place in perspective the contribution of the periphery to capital formation within Europe, O'Brien offers a number of propositions and quantifies their implications. Firstly, he takes an estimate that commodity trade with the periphery in 1800 accounted for perhaps 4 per cent of the aggregate gross national product of Western Europe. By the late eighteenth century, even in the maritime states of England, Portugal and the Netherlands, exports represented only about 10 per cent of gross national production with imports of a comparable proportion. Trade with the periphery represented less than half of those shares. To derive an estimate of the significance of trade with the periphery, O'Brien assumes that core capitalists enjoyed profits on the trade turnover of 50 per cent, a very generous estimate. He then assumes that these capitalists were extraordinarily thrifty, and reinvested 50 per cent of their profits. On these suppositions, the profits of trade with the periphery that were devoted to investment would have been only about 1 per cent of gross national product, or 10 per cent of gross investment. The latter category represents the sum of resources devoted to maintaining and increasing the stock of goods devoted to current and future production.

Trade with the periphery does not seem to have been especially profitable over the long term. The forces of competition always tend to press exceptional or 'super-normal' profits down to what is a normal rate of return on capital, allowing for risk. Trade with the periphery was generally subject to competition, despite mercantilist exclusiveness, and the initially high profits that flowed from the establishment of monopolies were competed away over time. The Iberian powers were only the earliest and most spectacular sufferers from this competitive process. Competition and its attendant lower prices benefited European consumers of exotic imports rather than the merchants.

There has been considerable but inconclusive debate about the effect of one egregious act of exploitation, the acquisition of precious metals from the Americas in the century following the Spanish conquest. The flow was likely to have been a stimulus to business, but the precise significance of the increased money supply in facilitating commerce and for the accumulation of capital is not clear, as O'Brien indicates. He emphasizes that in this period the earlier production of European mines, the development of financial instruments and institutions, and the debasement of currencies, all contributed to the increased availability of money needed in an expanding economy. Further, precious metals were useful in trade with the Baltic and the Orient, but they were perhaps not necessary for the former and imports from the Orient were largely luxuries. Finally, the extent to which American treasure contributed to rising prices in Europe is not clear, nor is the extent to which investment might have been stimulated by inflation-induced changes in wages, profit and rent. American treasure seems not to have been indispensable to European financial or economic development.

Those criticisms are consonant with the view of both Marxist and liberal historians, who consider that the development of capitalism within Europe was a sufficient cause of economic progress. The extra-European periphery may have been useful in the process, but it did not provide a necessary contribution. O'Brien's arguments to this effect are persuasive, often compelling, despite Wallerstein's reply (Wallerstein, 1983).

Although the economic development of Europe thus cannot be explained simply in terms of the exploitation of the New World and the Orient, the expanded trade, increased investment and widened commercial horizons that followed the Discoveries made *some* contribution to European economic growth. This is particularly so in relation to institutional change and to the importation of foodstuffs and raw materials. While O'Brien's work provides a valuable corrective to explanations of European development that are coloured by the glamour of oceanic trade or by the evils of exploitation, the dynamic effects of the geographical expansion of European activity and its indirect linkages are not necessarily captured by the arithmetic (Mathias, 1986: 52). Economic development occurs at the margin – no single element is likely to account for more than a few per cent of the total. O'Brien calculates that British trade with the periphery resulted in a level of gross annual investment at most 7 per cent higher than it would have been as a result of (hypothetical) alternative activities. However, the 7 per cent may have represented a significant increment in *net* investment, that is, the formation of productive assets above that necessary to preserve the existing stock intact. As Wallerstein puts it, 'every bit mattered' (1983: 528).

Wallerstein's model makes explicit the ways in which market imperfections and political power can and did distort the principle of all-round advantage that is associated with the free market. However, exploitation of the periphery by the core appears to account for little of European economic development; and that exploitation, whether by Europeans or the local elites symbiotic with them, may have contributed little to Oriental poverty. The enduring damage to the great civilizations of Asia seems to have been occasioned less by the maritime powers of Europe, the 'shipmen' as Mackinder (1919) called them in his geopolitical work, than by the 'horsemen', the nomad conquerors from the Central Asian steppe. The Mongols and their successors – Timur and his horde in Middle East, the Mughals in India, the Manchu in China – destroyed labour and capital, but the lasting deleterious effect of their domination of the rich and populous lands of Asia seems to have resulted more from the distorting political institutions they then imposed. Confronted by the rapacity of an elite ruling by right of conquest, the conquered tried to preserve what little remained to them by establishing or strengthening their own conservative institutions (Jones, 1988).

8

Review and preview

The models reviewed were each designed to explain how and why productivity changed over time. Economists conventionally specify the elements of the process as a production function, a functional relationship between input of factors of production – land, labour and capital – on one hand and output on the other. This serves for analysis of short-run production and distribution, but in analyses of long-term trends and levels of output other elements must be considered. These are technology, enterprise and the institutional structure; all are difficult to specify precisely and impossible to quantify. While any model can encompass only part of reality, those models which focus on only 'economic' factors are too limited to explain economic change. This is made clear if each factor of production is considered separately.

The factor of production land, or more broadly the environment, provides any given economy with a range of opportunities and costs. Thus its contribution to development can be assessed at least notionally. Further, if there is a change at the same time in the environment and in the economy, the direction of supposed causation is usually clear. However, explanations based on these considerations are necessarily incomplete: the economic significance of the principal components of the environment, location and resources, are themselves dependent on the availability of capital and the level of technology possessed by the society concerned or by its trading partners.

Labour, or more broadly population, has a double significance in analysis: people are both consumers and producers. Models dealing with this dual role of individuals may be illuminating but are not conclusive. In some circumstances population growth may be accompanied by Malthusian immiserization, in others by an intensification of production which when combined with innovation may hold the Malthusian spectre at bay for a considerable period or, in the more optimistic forecasts, indefinitely. In this, technical change and the availability of capital are again crucial variables.

The foregoing demonstrates the importance of capital accumulation and a changing technology in the process of economic development; but capital and technology do not of themselves provide an explanation for long-term change. Technical change can be shown to be largely a dependent variable, powerfully affecting productivity but itself a product of opportunities and incentives. Capital accumulation is similarly dependent upon inducements to invest that are reflections of economic and social conditions. Even investment in 'human capital', the term representing the health, skill and literacy of a workforce, is dependent on incentive and opportunity.

Because variations in the basic factors of production – land, labour and capital with technology – are partly the product of non-economic forces, some writers have looked to ideology as a motivator of human actions. Religion has been singled out for the most intensive study. Considerable attention has been given to the loose correlation between areas of economic development in early modern Europe and the areas that adopted Protestantism. This correlation is invested with causal significance by a model generally referred to as the Weber thesis.

In Weber's presentation (Collins, 1986), Protestant theology is seen as developing in its adherents a worldly as opposed to a monastic asceticism, a commitment to sobriety, diligence and thrift. With the Reformation came an accompanying 'spirit of capitalism' characterized by rational calculation in business rather than by speculation: in short, by a systematic pursuit of profit. The argument has been taken further, to find causation in the contemporaneous development of Protestantism and science (Webster, 1975). However, a historic relationship between Protestantism and economic development can be explained in a variety of non-theological ways (Kitch, 1967). Protestant business success, for example, can be related to the way in which members of a heterodox minority have perforce directed their energies towards commercial activity as a consequence of having been denied opportunity in the more prestigious occupations – the land, the law, government, the military, and of course the priesthood. This social phenomenon can also be seen historically without Protestantism in the cases of the Chinese in South East Asia, of the Parsees in India, of Indians in East Africa, of Armenians in the Islamic world and of Jews everywhere. In his later studies, Weber himself placed much less emphasis on the theological argument (Collins, 1986: 46). In any case, the model cannot account for the growth of the Japanese and other Confucian economies without straining beyond credulity. A more general criticism of explanations based on a particular culture is that they have difficulty in accounting persuasively for different rates of economic change in different periods.

The principal value of a model relating Protestantism to economic achievement lies not in its theological aspects, but in its drawing attention to the more general importance of the fragmentation of universalist intellectual and social structures. Protestantism was essentially individualistic. The Reformation destroyed the structure of uniform intellectual authority in Western Europe hitherto possessed by the Church. At the same time, the Renaissance enhanced individualism at the expense of the medieval corporate ideal. In this social climate, both scientific inquiry and market activity could flourish. Politically, the development of nation-states in Europe gave individualism greater scope: citizens had more opportunity in them of influencing policy – or of leaving – than they had in customary structures or would have had in an empire.

The emphasis on release from constraints points to a fruitful direction of research into why some societies experienced economic development and others did not. Work on that topic has generally been aimed at isolating and specifying whatever economic, or perhaps non-economic, variable was the cause of economic growth. This endeavour has been driven in recent decades by a need to define policy instruments that would alleviate poverty in the less developed areas of the world, and has been informed by two implicit assumptions. The first of these is that stagnation and poverty were normal conditions and economic growth was an aberration; while the second is that the Industrial

Revolution was the unique example of development. An alternative approach is to accept that economic growth is at least potentially a normal condition and to inquire why this potential has so seldom been realized.

Economic growth, in the sense of a sustained expansion of the economy roughly *pari passu* with an upward trend of population, appears to have been a general characteristic of change over time (Jones, 1989). In some places at some times – arguably in Tokugawa Japan, in Song dynasty China, in seventeenth-century Netherlands, and in eighteenth-century Britain – this simple economic expansion was translated into intensive growth, that is, into a sustained increase in *per capita* income resting on changes in technology and the institutional structure. Other than the British case, these phases of economic development have generally gone unremarked in growth studies as none led directly to industrialization. However, important as industrialization has been in changing the world, it is simply one expression of the process of economic development.

The foregoing examples of development, drawn from different places and periods, have a common element. They occurred when governmental constraints on economic activity were relaxed. In China, the Song emperors permitted the expansion of trade and the development of markets in a way extraordinary in Chinese history. They were seeking a new source of revenue from taxes on trade to offset the loss of land taxes to invaders who had occupied the northern provinces. Tokugawa Japan was a closely supervised police-state, but the central government was relatively indifferent to economic as opposed to political change, and allowed considerable autonomy to local areas and to merchants. The Dutch 'Golden Century' was based on commercial freedom and independence from the repressive power of Spain. In the Marxist schema, the bourgeois revolution in seventeenth-century England destroyed the constraints imposed by a decaying feudalism, the productive forces thus liberated leading to the Industrial Revolution; liberal historians tend to invest the Glorious Revolution of 1688 with a comparable significance. The liberalization of communist regimes in the Soviet Union and in Eastern Europe may have similar effects.

Broadly, the constraints on development that were imposed by governments flowed from their arbitrariness, rapacity, lethargy or their ineptness in economic matters. These behaviours inhibited the enterprise that seems to have existed to some extent in all large societies (Jones, 1988). Lethargic governments fail to provide the institutional or physical infrastructure useful for development, while ineptness results in counter-productive policies. Arbitrariness and rapacity were perhaps more serious failings of government, since in some circumstances private initiatives might have been able to provide elements of infrastructure neglected by government. Official rapacity at best deflected (to military purposes or conspicuous consumption) resources that might otherwise have been used to increase productivity. Rapacity combined with arbitrariness could eliminate any rational desire to accumulate assets in a productive form. In those risk-saturated circumstances, any surplus would be hoarded in the form of precious metals, or used by peasants to provide insurance in the form of additional children.

Elements of this argument were raised but overstated by Hicks in his broad condemnation of government activities. More circumspectly, North recognized that not all institutions have been such as to promote economic efficiency and development: some are designed to redistribute income rather than generate it. This point is the theme of Olson's explanation of stagnation (Olson, 1982).

In Olson's model, long periods of peace result in any economy becoming encrusted with institutions designed to benefit interest groups at the expense of the general welfare. Guilds and trade unions are chosen as historical and contemporary examples respectively. The post-war success of Germany and Japan is said to have followed from the destruction of conservative institutions in the traumas of dictatorship and military defeat. However, many aspects of historical stasis or change seem not to be within the purview of the model. For example, the power of guilds was sidestepped rather than shattered in some convulsion: merchants set up the 'domestic system', proto-industrial activity in the countryside beyond guild control. Again, the recovery of Germany and Japan after World War II had much to do with the quality of human capital that existed in each state, and with the policy of the United States to support post-war reconstruction in Western Europe and in non-communist Asian states. Moreover, while some countries were shattered by war yet enjoyed no comparable development, others, Switzerland and Sweden for example, escaped violent social and economic disruption but still prospered.

Each of the models reviewed in this survey contributes to an explanation of long-term change in large systems and offers a more or less comprehensive framework for understanding economic change. Each should be assessed in those terms. A model is neither 'right' nor 'wrong', except in the rigour of its logic, the accuracy of its facts, and the realism of its assumptions.[1] Assessment should focus on the comprehensiveness of the model and on its explanatory power. In this context, the inspiration of Kipling's Neolithic bard is illuminating:

> There are nine and sixty ways of
> constructing tribal lays,
> And every single one of them is right![2]

Models are in some respects like tribal lays, being more or less useful for particular purposes or more or less relevant to particular problems. The situation is succinctly summarized by North: 'to the degree that definitive tests of competing explanations are not possible there will be a number of scholarly explanations of the past – and theories to explain the present' (1981: 52).

In the construction of explanations for long-term economic change in large systems, attention is increasingly being paid to the restraints on growth rather than to the more traditional search for causes. Given this direction in research, increasing emphasis will probably be placed on the construction of models that specify constraints which inhibit economic development. These will necessarily incorporate institutional, political and ideological elements, as well as some that are 'economic' in a narrow sense. This new approach is unlikely to provide a definitive answer to the problem of explaining economic change over time. It may, however, narrow the range of explanations.

Notes

4 Population: the importance of people

1. McNeill has extended his analysis of parasite–host association beyond the 'micro-parasitism' of disease organisms to the 'macro-parasitism' historically common in political relationships (McNeill, 1979; 1980). These concepts reflect what are often said to be the only certainties of life: death and taxes.

2. These two seminal models have been synthesized into more complex generalized models of induced economic change (e.g. Pryor and Maurer, 1982; Coleman and Schofield, 1986).

5 Deus ex machina? Technology and science

1. Easterlin (1981) discusses the importance of education to the process of economic development. His thesis is supported by a study of Japan (Nakamura, 1981) but not by some other studies (e.g. Hanson, 1989).

2. Although a larger population statistically means that there will be more inventive people, realization of their potential depends on social institutions and the resources available to provide minimal nutrition, health and education. It is necessary to know whether the large population has adequate resources and appropriate institutions before it can be assumed that investment in 'human capital' will be forthcoming.

3. However, important as change in military technology was (Parker, 1988), many of the major developments in military systems seem not to have depended on technical change. The organization of the Roman legions, the emergence of the Mongol hordes, and the French innovation of a revolutionary 'nation in arms', as examples, were expressions more of social structures rather than of technical novelties.

8 Review and preview

1. The appropriateness of the last criterion has been disputed by Friedman (1953: *41*), who argues that the proper test of a model is its value in prediction.
2. 'In the Neolithic Age', *Rudyard Kipling's Verse. Definitive Edition* (New York, 1940).

Bibliography

This list is a guide only, being a selection of works dealing with long-term economic change. Further material may readily be found in the bibliographies of the works listed, and the indexes of journals, principally those devoted to economic history or economic development.

Items most useful as critiques of models considered in this book are marked with a star (*).

The date of first publication of a book, where this is significant, has been placed in square brackets after the author's name.

Anderson, J. L. (1981) 'History and Climate. Some Economic Models', in Wigley, T. N. L. *et al.* (eds), *Climate and History. Studies in Past Climates and their Impact on Man* (Cambridge).

Anderson, J. L. and Jones, E. L. (1988) 'Natural Diasasters and the Historical Response', *Australian Economic History Review*, 28:1.

Appleby, A. B. (1981) 'Epidemics and Famine in the Little Ice Age', in Rotberg, R. I. and Rabb, T. K. (eds), *Climate in History. Studies in Interdisciplinary History* (Princeton).

Aston, T. H. and Philpin, C. H. E. (eds) (1985) *The Brenner Debate: Agrarian Class Structure and Economic Development in Pre-Industrial Europe* (Cambridge).

Balazs, E. (1964) *Chinese Civilization and Bureaucracy. Variations on a Theme* (New Haven, Ct).

Basu, K., Jones, E. L. and Schlicht, E. (1987) 'The Growth and Decay of Custom: The Role of the New Institutional Economics in Economic History', *Explorations in Economic History*, 24.

(*)Bauer, P. T. (1971) 'Economic Theory as History', *Economica*, 38.

Boserup, E. (1965) *The Conditions of Agricultural Growth: the Economics of Agrarian Change under Population Pressure* (London).

Boserup, E. (1981) *Population and Technological Change: A Study in Long-Term Trends* (Chicago).

Boserup, M. (1964) 'Agrarian Structure and the Take-Off', in Rostow,

W. W. (ed.), *The Economics of Take-Off into Sustained Growth. Proceedings of a Conference held by the International Economics Association* (London).

Braudel, F. (1975) *The Mediterranean and the Mediterranean World in the Age of Philip II* (Glasgow).

Brenner, R. (1985) 'Agrarian Class Structure and Economic Development in Pre-Industrial Europe', in Aston, T. H. and Philpin, C. H. E. (eds), *The Brenner Debate: Agrarian Class Structure and Economic Development in Pre-Industrial Europe* (Cambridge).

(*)Brewer, A. (1980) *Marxist Theories of Imperialism: A Critical Survey* (Boston).

Bryson, R. A. and Murray, T. J. (1977) *Climates of Hunger. Mankind and the World's Changing Weather* (Canberra).

Cameron, R. (1989) *A Concise Economic History of the World from Paleolithic Times to the Present* (New York).

Carr, E. H. (1964) *What is History?* (Harmondsworth).

Cipolla, C. M. (1970) *European Culture and Overseas Expansion* (Harmondsworth).

(*)Coleman, D. and Schofield, R. (eds) (1986) *The State of Population Theory. Forward from Malthus* (Oxford).

Colinvaux, P. (1983) *The Fates of Nations. A Biological Theory of History* (Harmondsworth).

(*)Collins, R. (1986) *Weberian Sociological Theory* (Cambridge).

(*)Conway, D. (1987) *A Farewell to Marx. An Outline and Appraisal of his Theories* (Harmondsworth).

Crosby, A. W. (1972) *The Columbian Exchange. Biological and Cultural Consequences of 1492* (Westpoint, Ct).

Curtin, P. D. (1984) *Cross-Cultural Trade in World History* (Cambridge).

David, P. A. (1975) *Technical Choice, Innovation and Economic Growth. Essays on American and British Experience in the Nineteenth Century* (Cambridge).

David, P. A. (1986) 'Understanding QWERTY: the Necessity of History', in Parker, W. N. (ed.), *Economic History and the Modern Economist* (Oxford).

Davis, R. (1973) *The Rise of the Atlantic Economies* (London).

de Vries, J. (1976) *Economy of Europe in an Age of Crisis 1600–1750* (Cambridge).

de Vries, J. (1981) 'Measuring the Impact of Climate on History: The Search for Appropriate Methodologies', in Rotberg, R. I. and Rabb, T. K., *Climate and History. Studies in Interdisciplinary History* (Princeton, NJ).

Deane, P. (1965) *The First Industrial Revolution* (Cambridge).

Dodgshon, R. A. (1977) 'The Modern World-System: A Spatial Perspective', *Peasant Studies*, 6.

Easterlin, R. A. (1981) 'Why Isn't the Whole World Developed?', *Journal of Economic History*, 41.

Elvin, M. (1973) *The Pattern of the Chinese Past. A Social and Economic Interpretation* (Stanford).

Field, A. J. (1981) 'The Problem with Neoclassical Institutional Economics: A Critique with Special Reference to the North/Thomas Model of Pre-1500 Europe', *Explorations in Economic History*, 18.

Frank, A. G. (1967) *Capitalism and Underdevelopment in Latin America: Historical Studies of Chile and Brazil* (New York).

Friedman, M. (1953) *Essays in Positive Economics* (Chicago).

Galloway, P. R. (1986) 'Long-Term Fluctuations in Climate and Population in the Preindustrial Era', *Population & Development Review*, 12:1.

Gerschenkron, A. (1962) *Economic Backwardness in Historical Perspective. A Book of Essays* (Cambridge, Mass.)

Hahn, F. H. and Matthews, R. C. O. (1964) 'The Theory of Economic Growth', *The Economic Journal*, 74.

Hanson II, J. R. (1989) 'Education, Economic Development, and Technology Transfer: A Colonial Test', *Journal of Economic History*, 49.

Hicks, J. (1969) *A Theory of Economic History* (Oxford).

Hilton, R. H. and Sawyer, P. H. (1963) 'Technical Determinism: the Stirrup and the Plough', *Past and Present*, 24.

(*)Holton, R. J. (1985) *The Transition from Feudalism to Capitalism* (Houndmills).

Jones, E. L. (1981) *The European Miracle. Environments, Economies, and Geopolitics in the History of Europe and Asia* (Cambridge).

Jones, E. L. (1988) *Growth Recurring. Economic Change in World History* (Oxford).

Jones, E. L. (1989) 'Recurrent Transitions to *Intensive* Growth', in Goudsblom, J., Jones, E. L. and Mennell, S., *Human History and Social Process* (Exeter).

Kitch, M. J. (1967) *Capitalism and the Reformation* (London).

Kuhn, T. S. (1970) *The Structure of Scientific Revolutions* (Chicago).

Lamb, H. H. (1982) *Climate, History and the Modern World* (London).

Lane, F. C. (1958) 'Economic Consequences of Organized Violence', *Journal of Economic History*, 2nd Series, 28.

Lee, R. (1981) 'Short-Term Vital Rates, Prices and Weather', in Wrigley, E. A. and Schofield, R. S. *The Population History of England 1541–1871: A Reconstruction* (Cambridge, Mass.).

Mackinder, H. J. (1919) *Democratic Ideals and Reality: A Study in the Politics of Reconstruction* (London).

Malthus, T. R. (1970) [1798] *An Essay on the Principle of Population*; and *A Summary View of the Principle of Population*, ed. Flew, A. (Harmondsworth).

Marx, K. and Engels, F. (1967) [1848] *The Communist Manifesto*, ed. Taylor, A. J. P. (Harmondsworth).

Mathias, P. (1986) 'The Emergence of a World Economy 1500–1914', *Papers of the IX International Congress of Economic History Association* (Weisbaden).

Mayhew, N. C. and Tandy, D. W. (1985) 'Markets in the Ancient Near East: A Challenge to Silver's Argument and Use of Evidence', *Journal of Economic History*, 2nd Series, 45, with Silver's reply.

McClelland, P. D. (1975) *Causal Explanation and Model Building in History, Economics and the New Economic History* (Ithaca).

McCloskey, D. N. (1985) *The Rhetoric of Economics* (Madison).

McEvedy, C. and Jones, R. (1978) *Atlas of World Population History* (Harmondsworth).

McNeill, W. H. (1976) *Plagues and Peoples* (Harmondsworth).

McNeill, W. H. (1980) *The Human Condition. An Ecological and Historical View* (Princeton, NJ).

McNeill, W. H. (1982) *The Pursuit of Power. Technology, Armed Force, and Society since AD 1000* (Oxford).

Mennell, S. (1989) 'Bringing the Very Long Term back in', in Goudsblom, J., Jones, E. L. and Mennell, S., *Human History and Social Process* (Exeter).

Miskimin, H. A. (1977) *The Economy of Later Renaissance Europe 1460–1600* (Cambridge).

Mokyr, J. (1985) 'The Industrial Revolution and the New Economic History' in Mokyr, J. (ed.), *The Economics of the Industrial Revolution* (Totowa, NJ).

Nakamura, J. (1981) 'Human Capital Accumulation in Pre-Modern Rural Japan', *Journal of Economic History*, 41.

North, D. C. (1977) 'Markets and Other Allocation Systems in History: The Challenge of Karl Polanyi', *Journal of European Economic History*, 6:3.

North, D. C. (1981) *Structure and Change in Economic History* (New York).

North, D. C. (1984) 'Government and the Cost of Exchange in History', *Journal of Economic History*, 44.

North, D. C. and Thomas, R. P. (1970) 'An Economic Theory of the Growth of the Western World', *Economic History Review*, 2nd Series, 23.

North, D. C. and Thomas, R. P. (1973) *The Rise of the Western World. A New Economic History* (Cambridge).

North, D. C. and Weingast, B. R. (1989) 'Constitutions and Commitment. The Evolution of Institutions Governing Public Choice in Seventeenth-Century England', *Journal of Economic History*, 49.

(*)O'Brien, P. K. (1982) 'European Economic Development: The Contribution of the Periphery', *Economic History Review*, 2nd Series, 35.

Olson, M. (1982) *The Rise and Decline of Nations. Economic Growth, Stagflation and Social Rigidities* (New Haven, Ct).

Orwell, G. (1954) *Nineteen Eighty-four* (Harmondsworth).

Parker, G. (1988) *The Military Revolution. Military Innovation and the Rise of the West 1500–1800* (Cambridge).

Parker, G. and Smith, L. M. (1978) *The General Crisis of the Seventeenth Century* (London).

Parkinson, C. N. (1965) *East and West* (New York).

Parry, J. H. (1981) *The Age of Reconnaissance. Discovery, Exploration and Settlement 1450 to 1650* (Berkeley)

Perrin, N. (1980) *Giving up the Gun. Japan's Reversion to the Sword 1543–1879* (Boulder, Col.).

Polanyi, K. (1944) *The Great Transformation* (New York).

Pollard, S. (1981) *Peaceful Conquest. The Industrialization of Europe 1760–1970* (Oxford).

Pounds, N. J. and Ball, S. S. (1964) 'Core-Areas and the Development of the European States System', *Annals of the Association of American Geographers*, 54.

Pryor, F. L. and Maurer, S. B. (1982)'On Induced Economic Change in Precapitalist Societies', *Journal of Development Economics*, 10.

Rosenberg, N. (1976) *Perspectives on Technology* (Cambridge).

Rosenberg, N. (1982) *Inside the Black Box. Technology and Economics* (Cambridge).

Rostow, W. W. (1960) *The Stages of Economic Growth. A Non-Communist Manifesto* (Cambridge).

Rostow, W. W. (ed.) (1964) *The Economics of Take-Off into Sustained Growth. Proceedings of a Conference held by the International Economics Association* (London).

Rostow, W. W. (1975) *How It all Began. Origins of the Modern Economy* (New York).

Silver, M. (1983) 'Karl Polanyi and Markets in the Ancient Near East. The Challenge of the Evidence', *Journal of Economic History*, 2nd Series, 43.

Simon, J. L. (1977) *The Economics of Population Growth* (Princeton).

Simon, J. L. (1983) 'The Effects of Population on Nutrition and Economic Well-Being', *Journal of Interdisciplinary History*, 14:2.

Slicher van Bath, B. H. (1977) 'Agriculture in the Vital Revolution', in Rich, E. E. and Wilson, C. H. (eds) *The Cambridge Economic History of Europe*, Vol. 6 (Cambridge).

Smith, A. (1961) [1766] *An Inquiry into the Nature and Causes of the Wealth of Nations*, ed. E. Cannan (London).

Steensberg, A. (1951) 'Archaeological Dating of the Climatic Change in North Europe about AD 1300', *Nature*, 168.

Stover, L. E. and Stover, T. K. (1976) *China: An Anthropological Perspective* (Pacific Palisades, Cal.).

Szporluk, R. (1986) 'The Ukraine and Russia', in Conquest, R. (ed.), *The Last Empire. Nationality and the Soviet Future* (Stanford).

Tawney, R. (1938) *Religion and the Rise of Capitalism* (West Drayton, Middlesex).

Toynbee, A. J. (1934) *A Study of History* (London).

Unger, R. W. (1980) *The Ship in the Medieval Economy 600–1600* (Montreal).

Wallerstein, I. (1972) 'Three Paths of National Development in Sixteenth-Century Europe', *Studies in Comparative Economic Development*, 7:2.

Wallerstein, I. (1974a) *The Modern World-System. I. Capitalist Agriculture and the Origins of the European World-Economy in the Sixteenth Century* (Orlando, Fla.).

Wallerstein, I. (1974b) 'The Rise and Future Demise of the World Capitalist System', *Comparative Studies in Society and History*, 16.

Wallerstein, I. (1980) *The Modern World-System. II. Mercantilism and the Consolidation of the European World-Economy 1600–1750* (New York).

Wallerstein, I. (1983) 'European Economic Development: A Comment on O'Brien', *Economic History Review*, 2nd Series, 36, with O'Brien's reply.

Weber, M. (1968) [1904–5] *The Protestant Ethic and the Spirit of Capitalism* (London).

Webster, C. (1975) *The Great Instauration. Science, Medicine and Reform 1626/1660* (London).

White, C. M. (1987) *Russia and America: The Roots of Economic Divergence* (London).

White, Jr., L. (1962) *Medieval Technology and Social Change* (Oxford).

Wilson, C. (1965) *England's Apprenticeship 1603–1763* (London).

Winch, D. (1987) *Malthus* (Oxford).

Wittfogel, K. A. (1957) *Oriental Despotism: A Comparative Study of Total Power* (New Haven, Ct).

Index

New Studies in Economic and Social History

Titles in the series available from Cambridge University Press:

Previously published as

Studies in Economic History

Titles in the series available from the Macmillan Press Limited

Economic History Society

The Economic History Society, which numbers around 3,000 members, publishes the *Economic History Review* four times a year (free to members) and holds an annual conference.

Enquiries about membership should be addressed to

The Assistant Secretary
Economic History Society
PO Box 70
Kingswood
Bristol
BS15 5TB

Full-time students may join at special rates.